Tenerife

COLLINS
Glasgow & London

First published 1990
Copyright © William Collins Sons & Company Limited
Published by William Collins Sons & Company Limited
Printed in Hong Kong
ISBN 0 00 435784-1

HOW TO USE THIS BOOK

Your Collins Traveller Guide will help you find your way around your chosen destination quickly and easily. It is colour-coded for easy reference:

The blue-coded 'topic' section answers the question 'I would like to see or do something; where do I go and what do I see when I get there?' A simple, clear layout provides an alphabetical list of activities and events, offers you a selection of each, tells you how to get there, what it will cost, when it is open and what to expect. Each topic in the list has its own simplified map, showing the position of each item and the nearest landmark or transport access, for instant orientation. Whether your interest is Architecture or Sport you can find all the information you need quickly and simply. Where major resorts within an area require in-depth treatment, they follow the main topics section in alphabetical order.

The red-coded section is a lively and informative gazetteer. In one alphabetical list you can find essential facts about the main places and cultural items - 'What is La Bastille?', 'Who was Michelangelo?' - as well as practical and invaluable travel information. It covers everything you need to know to help you enjoy yourself and get the most out of your time away, from Accommodation through Babysitters, Car Hire, Food, Health, Money, Newspapers, Taxis and Telephones to Zoos.

Cross-references: Type in small capitals - CHURCHES - tells you that more information on an item is available within the topic on churches. A-Z in bold - **A-Z** - tells you that more information is available on an item within the gazetteer. Simply look under the appropriate heading. A name in bold - **Holy Cathedral** - also tells you that more information on an item is available in the gazetteer under that particular heading.

Packed full of information and easy to use - you'll always know where you are with your Collins Traveller Guide!

*Photographs by **James Carney***

If there's one thing better than a summer holiday in Tenerife it's a winter holiday there. Just a few hours after shedding warm woollies and wrenching yourself away from sub-zero temperatures you step off the aircraft not only in another continent but in a different climate. It's a place for all seasons - and all of them warm and welcoming. If you have no desire to return home bronzed, or sit at a seaside café at mid-night wearing only shorts and T-shirt, this is not the place for you. The temperature in winter 'falls' to 18°C. Little wonder that the Canaries are also referred to as the Fortunate Islands.

To a large extent, they have made their own fortune. The islands were born out of sub-sea volcanic eruptions so the land is barren rock and dust. However, around the resorts, a lot of hard work has gone into creating floral explosions of colour. Soil was imported, an intricate irrigation system set up, and plants which have pride of place in pots on window ledges in Britain grow wild in Tenerife as hedgerows. A stroll along the quiet backstreets is like walking through the most carefully cultivated of hothouses.

The other major attraction of Tenerife is that it is a duty-free island. The regional government of the Canaries recognises the earning potential of alcohol and tobacco and is dedicated to keeping costs down. This was a major factor in its refusal to become a fully integrated part of the Common Market. Locally-produced spirits cost about £3 a litre and cigarettes and excellent cigars can be purchased for pennies.

A word of warning: there the bargains end. The shops are crammed with cameras, watches, hi-fi and hi-tech gadgetry. The covers and cases carry the names of reputable manufacturers, but many are fakes, made in Far East countries. Examine the guarantee to discover the country of origin. Lace and leather goods are also plentiful, but prices vary from shop to shop. By all means express an interest with a trader, but look at what others are charging. Bartering is not welcomed, but prices can be reduced instantly by about ten per cent.

Hotels on the island are superb. Bedrooms are clean and spacious, swimming pools exciting and immaculately kept, and owners compete fiercely to create the most attractive reception areas and bars. The major emphasis is on marble, ponds and waterfalls, with many hotels proudly displaying plaques proclaiming the company which created the interior design. What's the food like? Well, Britons form a large percentage of tourists, so food is prepared to their tastes. There is also an appetizing selection of local dishes, each delightful to the palate. Apartments on the island are plentiful and pleasant, if functional, and most have their own swimming pools. The regional government of the island has decreed that the building of new hotels and apartments must be completed in a few years' time. That will be fine and dandy - in a few years' time. Now, however, a plethora of earth movers, diggers, shovellers and eaters is gouging huge holes into volcanic craters to prepare foundations. Acres of rock and dust are transformed into giant Legoland, with grey blocks sprouting where only cacti could survive. You could do worse than seek assurance from your travel agent or tour operator that the beautiful accommodation displayed in a glossy brochure is not next door to a building site.

Tenerife is dominated by Mount Teide, the 3718 m volcano in the centre of the island. Even in summer its peak, the highest on Spanish land, is snow-capped. A cable car will take you close to the summit and the fittest and keenest brave the climb in thin air to the top. From there, you can see the other islands in the Canaries and, it is said, a clear day reveals the coast of Africa. Then again, it is said that the celebrated dragon tree in Icod de los Vinos, a town at Teide's toes, is 3500 years old. How do they know? A tourists' guide confided 'It might be 350 years old. But 3500 years is better, yes?'.

There is a variety of trips and excursions available for the adventurer. The more energetic should take advantage of the water sports, including paragliding, windsurfing, water skiing and surfing. Then again, there is the sun and hundreds of delightful cafés. A final word of caution. It is easy and tempting to overindulge in amber rays or liquid. The results of both are painful. So relax and enjoy your stay!

William Coffey

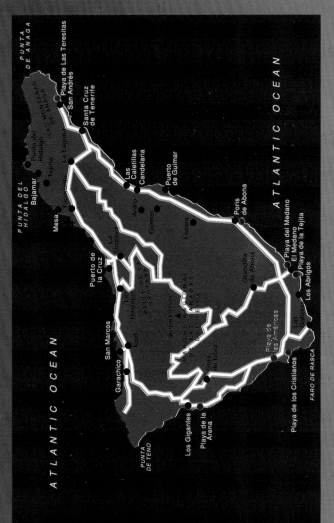

South & West

PLAYA DE LAS TERESITAS 9 km north-east of Santa Cruz.
San Andrés bus from Av Anaga, Santa Cruz.
Impressive artificial beach of golden sand. Calm bay, protected by stone dyke and palm trees. Popular with locals, but often quiet during the week.

PORIS DE ABONA 41 km south-west of Santa Cruz.
Bus 118, 130.
Medium sized bay of fine black sand. No facilities, and often crowded at weekends with families from Santa Cruz.

PLAYA DEL MÉDANO 60 km south-west of Santa Cruz.
Bus 116, 117 from Santa Cruz, 342 from Puerto de la Cruz.
Resort with a long stretch of yellow sand, near Reina Sofía (see **Airports***). Shallow water and exposed to the wind, therefore popular for surfing.*

PLAYA DE LA TEJITA 3 km south-west of El Médano.
Access via Playa del Médano.
A good sheltered beach on the south coast, set beneath the small rocky outcrop of Montaña Roja.

PLAYA DE LOS CRISTIANOS 75 km south-west of Santa Cruz.
Bus 111 from Santa Cruz.
Stretches of soft brown sand protected by jetties, near the busy ferry port of this tourist resort. Beach equipment for hire and water sports available. A safe haven for children.

PLAYA DE LAS AMÉRICAS 3 km north-west of Los Cristianos.
Bus 111 from Santa Cruz.
Varied beaches with hard sand, grainy sand, pebbles and rocks strung along the tree-lined promenade. All water sports equipment available for hire.

PLAYA DE LA ARENA 30 km north-west of Los Cristianos.
Access from Puerto de Santiago.
A bay of fine black sand, steeply sloping underwater, with rocks to either side. Overlooked by a terraced restaurant and with a good view of Gomera (see **EXCURSION 5, ISLANDS, A-Z***).*

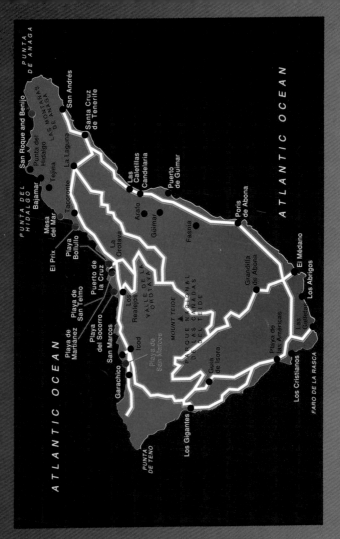

North

SAN ROQUE AND BENIJO 2-4 km north-east of Taganana.
*Scenic beaches with big waves and a strong undertow. Don't swim too far,
but have fun building an appetite before heading for the beach restaurants.*

MESA DEL MAR 7 km north of Tacoronte.
TF 122 from Tacoronte. Turn left after 4 km.
*A recent tourist development on the rugged northern coastline, offering
a good small beach of black sand, set beneath steep cliffs.*

EL PRIX 8 km north of Tacoronte, next to Mesa del Mar.
TF 122 from Tacoronte. Turn left after 4 km.
*Charming fishing port, with a small beach of fine black sand and good
restaurants, but no amenities. A favourite amongst the locals.*

PLAYA BOLLULLO Beach road north of Puerto de la Cruz.
30 min walk from centre of Puerto de la Cruz.
*Lovely, secluded little beach for those seeking peace and quiet. Lacking in
amenities but good for swimming.*

PLAYA DE MARTIÁNEZ Av de Colón, Puerto de la Cruz.
*A small bay of black sand with a rock jetty providing protection from the
waves and wind, and with restaurants nearby.*

PLAYA DE SAN TELMO c/ San Telmo, Puerto de la Cruz.
*Not a beach as such, but fun to look down from Calle de San Telmo and
watch the waves break dramatically over the rocky promontory. See* **WALK 3**.

PLAYA DEL SOCORRO 8 km west of Puerto de la Cruz.
C 820 from Puerto de la Cruz, turn off at Los Realejos.
Isolated beach with tapas huts (see **Food***) and a natural shower formed by
a cascading freshwater spring. Currents can make swimming treacherous.*

PLAYA DE SAN MARCOS 24 km west of Puerto de la Cruz.
C 820 from Puerto de la Cruz, turn off at Icod.
*Medium sized bay of dark fine sand and clear water, surrounded by rugged
cliffs offering a beautiful view over the sea.*

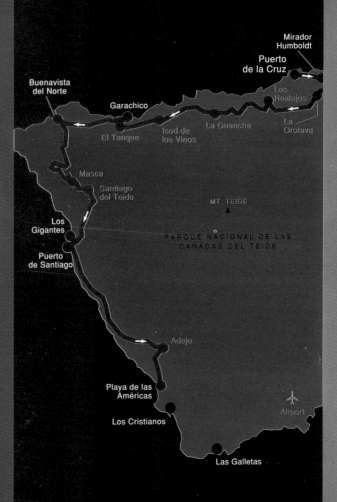

121 km. *A one-day excursion exploring the area around La Orotava, Icod, Masca and Los Gigantes.*

Puerto de la Cruz. From the centre of town follow the signs for the motorway to Santa Cruz and after about 3 km take the exit for La Orotava climbing up near the Mirador Humboldt.

8 km - La Orotava. A sedate town and one of the oldest in Tenerife. Follow your way up through the shops in the newer part of town, bearing right to pass the 18thC cathedral, Nuestra Señora de la Concepción (see **WHAT TO SEE 4**, **A-Z**) and then along the Calle San Francisco where you pass the Casa de los Balcones with its embroidery school (see **WHAT TO SEE 4**). Arriving at the Plaza San Francisco, enjoy the view over La Orotava valley from the Hospital de la Santísima Trinidad (see **WHAT TO SEE 4**). Continue up out of town to take the Los Realejos road through the scattered dwellings. See **A-Z**.

16 km - Los Realejos. Once two villages used as camps by the opposing forces of the Guanches (see **A-Z**) and Conquistadores, and the site of Tenerife's last battle, at the end of the 15thC (see **A-Z**). Follow the signs for La Guancha on TF 221, climbing through Tigaiga and Icod de Alto, offering good views of the valley, before arriving at La Guancha itself, a typical Canarian village. Turn right to rejoin the C 280, then bear left towards Icod.

39 km - Icod de los Vinos (see **A-Z**). Bear right through the town until you see the Playa de San Marcos (see **BEACHES 2**) sign-posted on the right, and turn left towards the impressive dragon tree, Drago of Icod (see **WHAT TO SEE 4**, **A-Z**), and the beautiful church of San Marcos nearby (see **WHAT TO SEE 4**). You may wish to stop for a typical Canarian lunch at Carmen's (see **RESTAURANTS 3**). Continue past the dragon tree along the C 820. At 6 km, past San Juan del Reparo, turn right towards Garachico and wind your way down the hairpin bends, resisting the superb views until you reach Tanque, where it is safe to stop. Continue past Las Cruces and San Pedro de Daute.

54 km - Garachico. A pleasant town that was almost completely destroyed by the 1706 eruption of Volcán de Negro, and was rebuilt on a semi-circular mass of cooled lava. Visit the natural rock swimming pools and the Castillo de San Miguel (1000-1900 daily), a 16thC

fortress which survived the volcanic eruption. Embroidery and other souvenirs are on sale. See **A-Z**.

63 km - Buenavista (see **A-Z**). The most north-westerly village in Tenerife. A calm place with beautiful views and a 16thC church, Virgen de los Remedios, which houses a fine painting of St Francis. Take the road opposite the petrol station, heading for El Palmar, and start climbing into the Teno massif region. The views along the Valle del Palmar are breathtaking and the island of Gomera (see **ISLANDS**, **EXCURSION 5**, **A-Z**) is visible off the coast. The road narrows after El Palmar.

76 km - Masca. A tiny village spread out at the top of a gorge and formerly known as the 'hidden village' due to its inaccessibility. Masca is now on the tourist trail, but retains much of its original identity. Continue south, climbing out of the gorge. At 6 km stop at the lay-by to marvel at the wonderful views of the sea on the right and Mount Teide (see **EXCURSION 2**, **A-Z**) on the left. Then the road drops down steeply into Santiago del Teide. Turn right along the C 820 and the road continues to twist and turn, albeit less dramatically, and then turn right at Tamaimo to take the TF 1480 towards Los Gigantes.

92 km - Los Gigantes (see **A-Z**). Turn right down the town's one-way system and descend towards the pleasant marina and stop to browse through the shops or admire the awesome serenity of the cliffs. On the way up back out of town, just beyond the taxi rank, stop off for a refreshment and savour the atmosphere of one of the resort's oldest establishments, the aptly named Bamboo Bar. Continue out of town and turn right for the short journey to Puerto de Santiago.

94 km - Puerto de Santiago. A tasteful little resort with a small bay of black sand, Playa de la Arena (see **BEACHES 1**), overlooked by a restaurant. Rejoin the main road south by turning right 2 km out of the village and enjoy the less dramatic scenery of the west coast.

114 km - Adeje. An attractive little village, best known as the starting point of the walk down the Barranco del Infierno (see **A-Z**). On its main street is the 17th/18thC church, Iglesia de Santa Úrsula.

121 km - Playa de las Américas. Return to the C 822 main road towards this coastal resort (see **BEACHES 1**, **A-Z**), which marks the end of this excursion.

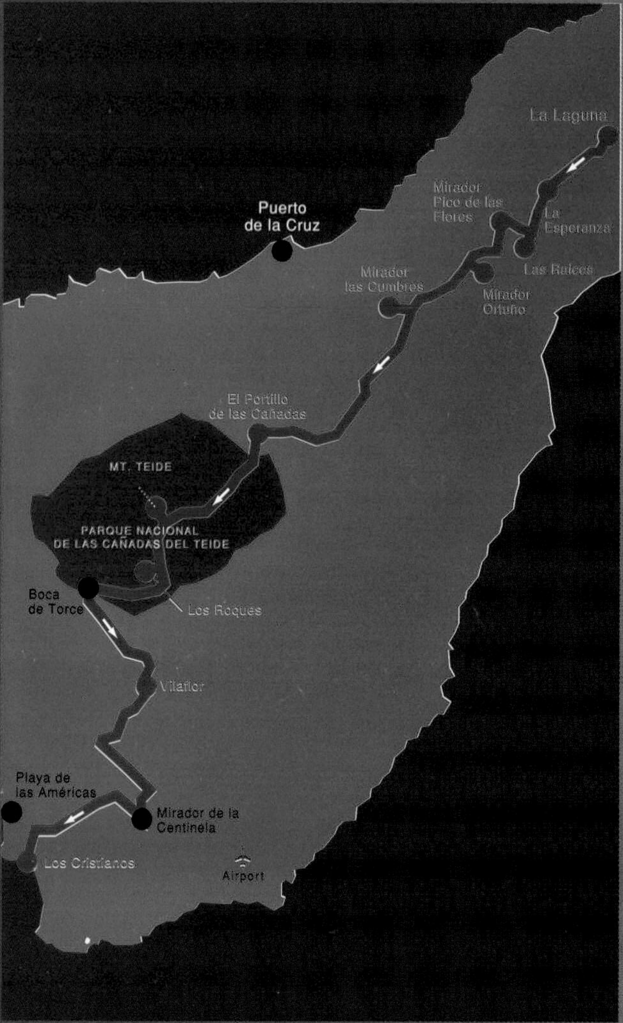
La Laguna
Mirador Pico de las Flores
La Esperanza
Puerto de la Cruz
Las Raíces
Mirador las Cumbres
Mirador Ortuño
El Portillo de las Cañadas
MT. TEIDE
PARQUE NACIONAL DE LAS CAÑADAS DEL TEIDE
Boca de Torce
Los Roques
Vilaflor
Playa de las Américas
Mirador de la Centinela
Los Cristianos
Airport

Mount Teide

100 km. *A one-day excursion across Tenerife from Santa Cruz to Los Cristianos via Mount Teide.*

7 km - La Laguna. Turn off the *autopista* from Santa Cruz at the signs for La Laguna University. Turn left at the first roundabout to take the C 824 leading inland through gently undulating pasture land to the town of La Esperanza. The road begins to wind upwards along the spine of the island, with views of the sea off both coasts.

13 km - La Esperanza. Quite suddenly you enter La Esperanza Forest (see **A-Z**). Continue climbing through its magnificent greenery. Turn left after about 1 km just in front of the Bar las Raíces café.

17 km - Las Raíces. A few hundred metres along the track there is a clearing among the tall pine trees in the middle of which stands the historical monument of Las Raíces (see **A-Z**). Return to the C 824.

20 km - Mirador Pico de las Flores. After a sharp bend to the right, you come to this mirador, with an impressive view over the south-easterly slopes, and a sight of Santa Cruz in the distance. The road then straightens and levels out, and you'll find yourself driving through young silver eucalyptus trees and shrubs.

27 km - Mirador Ortuño. The next stop is the Mirador Ortuño which offers a splendid panorama of the northern coast and its resorts. Shortly afterwards you catch glimpses, and then the full view, of Mount Teide (see **WALK 4**, **A-Z**). Take a detour to the right after 6 km and join the small road leading to the Mirador las Cumbres.

35 km - Mirador les Cumbres. From here you can fully appreciate the snow-capped splendour of the mountain. Return to the C 824. At an altitude of 2000 m the forest ends, revealing a landscape of purple brown earth dotted with *retama* (broom). Pass the Izaña Metereological station to your left and continue on to El Portillo.

54 km - El Portillo de las Cañadas. Turn left here, and then on your right, shortly after the junction and set back slightly from the road, is the Centro de Visitantes (open 0900-1600) covering the geology, history and biology of the Parque Nacional del Teide (see **A-Z**), with slides and specimens and a video room running programmes in English (every hour on the half hour). Continue your journey through the strange lunar landscape of the area. Turn right after 11 km.

65 km - Mount Teide Cable Car. The cable car takes visitors towards the peak of the Mount Teide volcano and there is also a restaurant offering expensive lunches. Back on the C 821, you pass the *parador* on the left (see **Accommodation**), and the turning on the right leads you to the strange rock formations known as Los Roques.

69 km - Los Roques. From here you have extensive views of the crater below. As you continue towards the edge of the crater, notice the blue rock through which the road cuts, and the mysterious columns of rock which rise out of the crater wall. After about 7 km bear left at the junction to take the C 821. Once you cross the outer ridge, the landscape drops steeply away to the right as you descend through pine forests towards Vilaflor.

81 km - Vilaflor. At 1400 m, this is the highest village in Spain and is famous for the purity of its water. Set in neat terraced vineyards and almond trees, it offers peace and quiet and contains good examples of typical Canarian architecture. Follow the signs to Arona and Los Cristianos by turning right just outside the village.

100 km - Los Cristianos. The road offers a panoramic view of the arid plains and volcanic outcrops of the south, with the airport on your left and the beach resorts of Los Cristianos (see **A-Z**) and Playa de las Americás (see **A-Z**) behind the hills on your right.

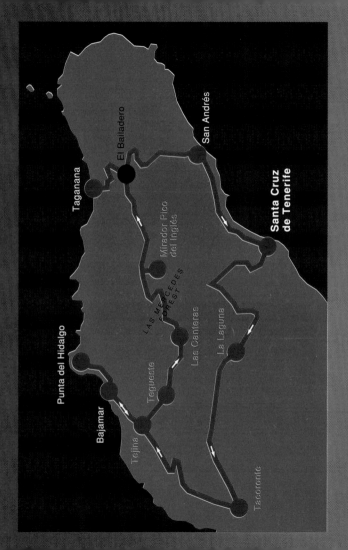

Anaga Mountains

102 km. *A one-day round trip from Santa Cruz through the mountainous region in the north-eastern tip of the island.*

7 km - La Laguna (see **WALK 2**, **WHAT TO SEE 2**, **A-Z**). The *autopista* or the C 824 from Santa Cruz takes you the short distance to this, the university town of Tenerife and the island's first capital. The streets are designed on a grid system. Take time to wander through the town and appreciate the many fine examples of Canarian architecture, and stop to admire La Laguna Cathedral and the Iglesia de Nuestra Señora de la Concepción. The C 820 out of town takes you past Guamasa towards Tacoronte.

17 km - Tacoronte. Formerly a capital of the Guanches (see **A-Z**). Turn right to descend out of the centre of town and notice the fine *drago* on the right (see **A-Z**). The junction to the left of the tree takes you towards the older part of town where there are two fine examples of 16th and 17thC churches, Iglesia de Santa Catalina and Iglesia del Cristo de los Dolores, the latter housing a much venerated, sacred image of Christ (see **WHAT TO SEE 4**, **A-Z**). Return to the junction and take the Tejina road along the TF 122. Just out of Tacoronte look for a sign on the left for the Museo Etnográfico (Casa de Carta), and turn left down the car park on the far side of the building (see **WHAT TO SEE 4**). Continue through the banana plantations of Valle de Guerra for 10 km to Tejina, where you bear left for Bajamar at the roundabout.

30 km - Bajamar (see **A-Z**). A popular and relaxing seaside resort, well known for its tidal swimming pools. A picturesque place and ideal spot to have lunch. Turn left out of the resort.

33 km - Punta del Hidalgo. The road ends here at a roundabout from where you can see the village's small rocky beach and the rugged cliffs cutting into the sea. Return to the roundabout at Tejina (6 km) and turn left along the TF 121 which snakes up through eucalyptus and tamarisk trees to Tegueste (3 km). Continue on to Las Canteras (4 km), driving slowly in order to take a sharp U-turn to the left at the junction in the centre of the village, onto the TF 114.

48 km - Las Mercedes. Climb up into Las Mercedes Forest through cedars and then laurel trees intermingled with briar. As you travel along the ridge which divides the island in two, both coasts become visible. Follow the signs for the Mirador Pico del Inglés.

55 km - Mirador Pico del Inglés. From here, at an altitude of 992 m, you can look down into the tree-clad Afur valley, often thinly veiled in a fine mist. Return from this 1 km detour and turn right to rejoin the road past Las Casas de la Cumbre. The road initially has a good surface and passing places, though it becomes narrower as you descend. At the foot (11 km) go straight on, following the signs for Taganana and San Andrés, and then turn left after 2 km to take the Taganana road along the TF 1124. The road takes you through a tunnel and down some steep hair-pin bends.

72km - Taganana. An extremely picturesque settlement (one of the oldest on the island), with the Roque de las Ánimas in the distance. It is worth continuing on to the Playa del Roque (2 km) for a swim or refreshment in one of the roadside bars, or just to admire its romantic scenery (see **BEACHES 2**). Return to Taganana (2 km) and turn left at the junction to take the San Andrés and Santa Cruz road affording good views of the cliffs and sea, again watching out for a series of tight bends.

93 km - San Andrés. Here it is possible to take a short detour to the left and visit Tenerife's artificially created beach of golden sand, Playa de las Teresitas (see **BEACHES 1**), and then return to follow the route to Santa Cruz along the TF 111.

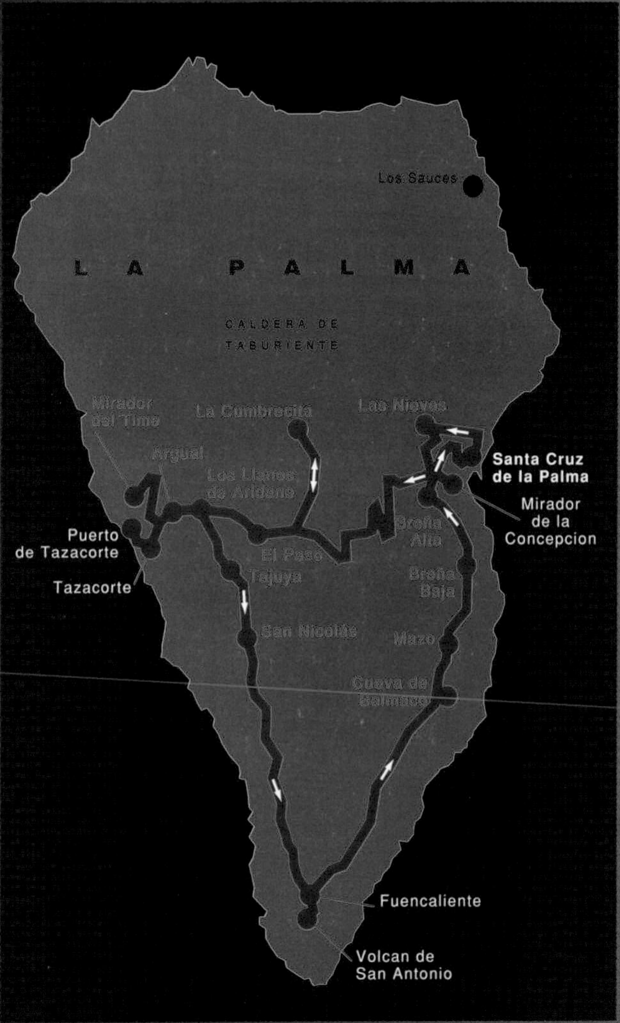

LA PALMA

CALDERA DE
TABURIENTE

Los Sauces

Mirador
del Time

La Cumbrecita

Las Nieves

Argual

Los Llanos
de Aridane

Santa Cruz
de la Palma

Mirador
de la
Concepcion

Puerto
de Tazacorte

El Paso
Tajuya

Breña
Alta

Tazacorte

Breña
Baja

San Nicolás

Mazo

Cueva de
Belmaco

Fuencaliente

Volcan de
San Antonio

La Palma

130 km. *A one-day tour around the most fertile and one of the most beautiful of the Canary Islands. See* **ISLANDS, A-Z**.

From Santa Cruz de la Palma take the road leading north and turn first left to climb steeply up from the coast.

5 km - Las Nieves. Built on the side of the mountain. The village church houses the jewelled 14thC statue of the island's patron saint, Nuestra Señora de las Nieves. Every five years *La Bajada de la Virgen* (The Descent of the Virgin) is celebrated, and the statue is carried to Santa Cruz in a procession of floats representing miraculous interventions of the saint. Continue south along the C 830, stopping after 5 km at the Mirador de la Concepción with its splendid view of the coast and Santa Cruz. Take the inland route heading for El Paso along the TF 812. The road climbs the eastern slopes of the mountains before a tunnel provides access to the other side. Turn right 4 km after the tunnel.

34 km - La Cumbrecita. At 1833 m, this is a natural balcony which offers wonderful views of La Caldera de Taburiente, notably at the Mirador Lomo de las Chozas. The peaks of the ridge of this enormous crater can be seen opposite, and above rises the Roque de los Muchachos which, at 2426 m, is the highest point of the island. The monolithic rock called Idafe, which was an object of worship for the Guanches (see **A-Z**), can be seen rising from the floor of the crater. Retrace your route back to the TF 812 and turn right to drive through pine forests and almond groves.

46 km - El Paso. A centre of silk-making and of the local brand of cigars, Capote. The town is set amongst almond groves which attract numerous visitors when the trees blossom in February. Take the road to Los Llanos de Aridane past plantations of bananas.

50 km - Los Llanos de Aridane. The island's second town, an agricultural centre surrounded by banana plantations and almond groves. Take the C 832 to cross the valley and turn right at Argual. Every inch of the steep slopes has been used for banana cultivation. Note the irrigation channels clinging to the sides of the mountains.

61 km - Mirador del Time. This offers a panoramic view of the terraces of the valley of Aridane, the most beautiful valley of the island, and of the Barranco de las Angustias. Return to the C 832 and turn right on the

other side of the gorge, before Argual.

72 km - Tazacorte. A centre of banana cultivation. Visit La Casa de los Mártires, which commemorates the life of the Jesuit missionary, Father Azevedo, killed by Huguenot privateers, 15 July, 1570. From Puerto de Tazacorte (3 km) you can take a boat trip to the Cueva Bonita, an attractive cave with strange effects of blue light (1 hr to the north, 1500 ptas). Puerto de Tazacorte is a popular resort with the locals and ideal for a lunch of fresh grilled fish. It is also of historical interest, for here the invading Spanish forces, led by Alonso Fernández de Lugo (see **A-Z**), landed in 1492. Return to Los Llanos and take the C 832 towards the south of the island, past Tajuya and San Nicolás. The region was affected by a volcanic eruption in 1949 which divided the village of San Nicolás in two and left a startling legacy of lava fields.

101 km - Fuencaliente. This southernmost town is a wine-producing centre and here you can sample the finest *malvasía* in the island (see **Drinks**). The town was a former hot water spa until the source was destroyed by the 1677 eruption of the San Antonio volcano. Take a detour (1 km south) to climb up to the craters (last active in 1971) and survey the surrounding countryside, still covered in ash yet already being cultivated. Take the C 832 through fields of lava and past a pine forest on the left. Fork right at Tigalate and drive along the fertile coastal strip with its steep cliffs.

115 km - Cueva de Belmaco. The dwelling-place of the last native king of Tigalete. The significance of the cave lies in its prehistoric spiral inscriptions, which are as yet undeciphered but may turn out to be a form of writing.

119 km - Mazo. A charming village of whitewashed houses which line the steep streets and alleys. Beautiful 16thC statues of the Virgin are housed in the Iglesia de San Blas, behind which is an atelier where you can watch girls embroidering in the cool patio. Continue north along the winding road towards the village of Breña Baja, turning left to reach Breña Alta.

130 km - Breña Alta. Famous for its plaited palm work and as a source of mineral water. Just before entering the village, notice its twin *dragos* (see **A-Z**) on the left, in San Isidro. Follow signs for Santa Cruz de la Palma (11 km).

Gomera

126 km. *A one-day excursion around the small and lush island to the west of Tenerife. See* **ISLANDS, A-Z.**

San Sebastián. The capital of the island with a population of 7000, and notable as a port of call for Christopher Columbus (see **A-Z**). Visit the Torre del Conde, a 15thC fortified tower (and now a museum) where Beatriz de Bobadilla (see **A-Z**) took refuge from the rebellious Guanches (see **A-Z**). The Iglesia de la Asunción houses a 19thC fresco depicting the 1599 attack on Gomera by the Dutch. Columbus resided for a time in the Casa de Colón in the charming main street of the town.

Leave San Sebastián by the main road north-west along the Barranco Seco (TF 711) to discover a pleasant countryside of terraces and orchards. Then pass through the Túnel del Cumbre and arrive at the beautiful Valle de Hermigua. The road then descends towards the northern coast of the island.

23 km - Hermigua. A town of 6000 inhabitants and built on the slopes of the Barranco de Monteforte. Visit the two churches or swim at the pretty La Caleta beach east of the town, which has good views of Tenerife. From the beach it is possible to hire a boat to visit Los Órganos, impressive basalt columns which lie just north of Puerto de Vallehermoso.

27 km - Agulo. A village in a picturesque setting, surrounded by high cliffs. Visit Los Telares, just before the village, and see the women weaving.

42 km - Vallehermoso. An agricultural centre dominated by El Roque Cano, an imposing basalt rock formed by the erosion of the surrounding lava. Continue along the TF 711, winding through broom and pine forests and then descend past the palm groves after Arure, offering a splendid view over the canyon, and village of Taguluche to your right.

68 km - Valle Gran Rey. The most beautiful valley of the island, revealing different glimpses of scenery at each twist of the road. Majestic mountain countryside of terraced slopes and palm trees.

74 km - Vueltas. A small port at the foot of cliffs where you can have a leisurely lunch of seafood. Boats leave from here for Playa de Santiago. You might feel like a swim at the Playa de Calera, 2.5 km to the north.

Return through the Valle Gran Rey, then turn off to the right after about 18 km along the TF 713, between Arure and Vallehermosa. Take the next right-hand fork to follow the road to Las Hayas and El Cercado.

97 km - El Cercado. The pottery made in this and other local villages is collectively known as *Chipude*, and in the workshops it is still possible to see potters at work.

Continue on to Temocoda (1 km) and then bear left and almost immediately right to take the road that leads to the outskirts of the Parque Nacional de Garajonay. At Igualero (6 km), take the junction to the left and at the following junction (1 km) take the road to the right leading back to San Sebastián (21 km).

GRAN CANARIA

The capital is Las Palmas. The countryside is characterized by lush vegetation, gorges and volcanic areas. Regular flights and ferries to the other islands. See **A-Z**.

FUERTEVENTURA

The capital is Puerto del Rosario. Fuerteventura is only 90 km from the African coast and features African flora and sandy beaches. Frequent flights and ferries to La Palma and Lanzarote. See **A-Z**.

LA PALMA

The capital is Santa Cruz de la Palma. The island features one of the earth's biggest craters, the Caldera de Taburiente, (800 m deep, 10 km wide). It is the most luxuriant of the islands. Daily flights and frequent ferry services. See **EXCURSION 4**, **A-Z**.

LANZAROTE

The capital is Arrecife. It retains the most recent effects of volcanic activity and features a strange but beautiful lunar landscape. Camels are used to work the fields. Regular flights and ferry services to other islands. See **A-Z**.

TENERIFE

The largest of the islands in the Canaries, the capital is Santa Cruz de Tenerife. The island has an extremely varied geography and climate. Daily flights to the continent as well as numerous charter flights. Regular flights and hydrofoil and ferry links to the other islands. See **Orientation**.

GOMERA

The capital is San Sebastián. The only island with no recent volcanic activity. It possesses beautiful forests and some picturesque beaches. Daily and weekly ferry links with other islands. See **EXCURSION 5**, **A-Z**.

HIERRO

The capital is Valverde. The westernmost of the islands, and the smallest, Hierro is extremely beautiful and thus far unexploited by tourism. Daily flights to Tenerife and regular ferry links. See **A-Z**.

Santa Cruz

DAIDA Edfo Daida, c/ Carlos J. R. Hamilton.
•2200-0430 Mon.-Fri., 2200-0530 Sat., 1900-0430 Sun. •600-800ptas.
Biggest disco in Santa Cruz. Varied music, three bars and plenty of seating.

TROPO Rambla del General Franco, 96.
•2300-0500 Sun.-Thurs., 2300-0630 Fri. & Sat. •700ptas.
Stylish, formal but friendly disco with video screens and two bars.

PIMS c/ Bethencourt Alfonso, off Pza de España.
•1900-0200 Fri.-Sun. •300ptas (drinks 150ptas).
Funky disco with young clientele. Informal and lively.

TORMENTÍN Edfo Los Delfines, c/ Carlos J. R. Hamilton.
•2000-0030 Mon.-Sat. •Entry free, drinks 150-300ptas.
Young clientele, simple decor, modern music, video screen and pinball.

SAXO PUB c/ Calvo Sotelo, off Rambla del General Franco.
•1930-0230. •Entry free, drinks 125-300ptas.
Black and orange decor. Friendly atmosphere, Spanish and funky music.

TINABANA Edfo Mabel, Centro Res Anaga, 14.
•0800-0200. •Entry free, drinks 300-500ptas.
Elegant decor, varied clientele. Also has a restaurant, terrace and piano bar.

BAR COLONIAL c/ Candelaria, 12.
•1000-1300 & 1800-2300 Mon.-Sat. •Entry free.
Small but fascinating local bar with a multitude of curios hanging from the ceiling and decorating the patio. See **WALK 1**.

CAFÉ DEL PRÍNCIPE Pza del Príncipe.
•0900-2400 Tues.-Sat. •Entry free.
Charming, quiet terrace bar under park trees, in keeping with 19thC style.

VIVA MARÍA c/ Suárez Guerra, 20.
•0900-2400. •Juices/Sandwiches 150ptas.
The best fruit juices in town and a tasty selection of toasted sandwiches.

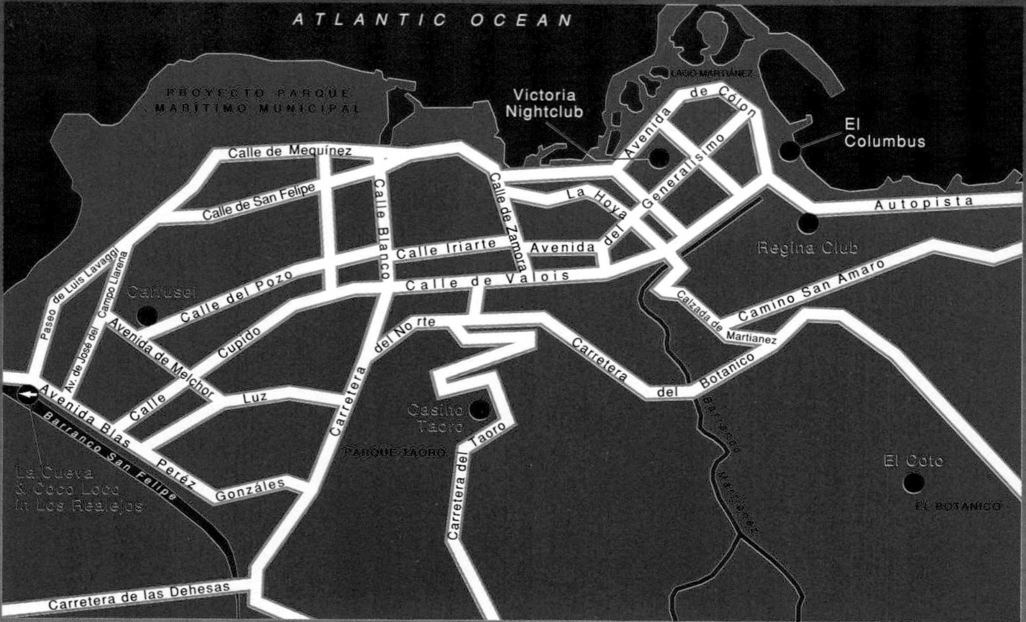
ATLANTIC OCEAN
PROYECTO PARQUE MARITIMO MUNICIPAL
LAGO MARTIÁNEZ
Victoria Nightclub
El Columbus
Avenida de Cólon
Generalísimo
Autopista
Regina Club
Calle de Mequínez
Calle de San Felipe
Calle Blanco
Calle de Zamora
La Hoya
Avenida del
Calle Iriarte
Avenida
Calle de Valois
Camino San Amaro
Calzada de Martianez
Carrusel
Calle del Pozo
Paseo de Luis Lavaggi
Av. de José del Campo Llarena
Avenida de Melchor
Cupido
Calle
Luz
Carretera del Norte
Carretera del Botanico
Barranco Martianez
Casino Taoro
PARQUE TAORO
Carretera del Taoro
Avenida Blas Peréz Gonzáles
Barranco San Felipe
La Cueva & Coco Loco in Los Realejos
Carretera de las Dehesas
El Coto
EL BOTANICO

REGINA CLUB Oro Negro Hotel, Av de Colón, 14.
•2200-0400. •3000ptas.
A magnificent disco with up-market clientele, and containing an underwater ballet show visible through a window behind the bar.

LA CUEVA La Languera, 4 km west of Puerto de la Cruz.
•2000-0300. •3900ptas.
Restaurant on a cliff with views of the sea. International entertainment in a Guanche (see A-Z) setting. African and flamenco dancing. See Excursions.

CASINO TAORO Parque de Taoro.
•2000-0300. Free taxi service from town. •500ptas.
Roulette, blackjack, other table games and slot machines, with restaurant and bar. Formal dress. Passport or ID card obligatory. Minimum age 18.

EL COLUMBUS Av de Colón, 2.
•1800-0200.
Piano bar downstairs and a disco upstairs, attracting a select clientele.

EL COTO Hotel Botánico, Av Richard J. Yeoward.
•2200-0430 Sun.-Thurs., 2200-0630 Fri. & Sat. •600ptas.
Jazz, salsa and disco music attracts a young fashionable crowd to this stylish disco with elegant tropical decor.

VICTORIA NIGHTCLUB Bajos Hotel, Av de Colón.
•2200-0430. •600ptas.
Piano bar with terrace looking out over the sea. Disco in basement playing slow music for mature clientele.

COCO LOCO Hotel Maritim, El Burgado, Los Realejos.
•2000-0400. •800ptas.
Elegant disco and bands playing requests. Popular with the older age group.

CARRUSEL Edfo Valle Luz, Av de Melchor Luz.
•2200-0400. •600ptas.
The latest in modern international music, with young lively clientele.

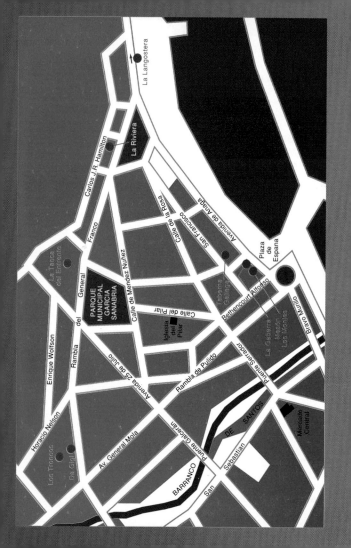

Santa Cruz

LA RIVIERA Rambla del General Franco, 155.
•1200-1500 & 2000-2400 Mon.-Sat. •Expensive.
Top quality French cuisine with excellent service in elegant surroundings.

TABERNA GALLEGA c/ San Francisco, 38.
•1300-1600 & 2000-2400 Mon.-Sat. •Moderate-Expensive.
Small family establishment serving fish of your own choice from northern Spain. Fishing boat decor.

LA GABARRA c/ Emilio Calzadilla, 3.
•1200-1600 & 2000-2400 Mon.-Sat. •Moderate.
Surprisingly plain decor but excellent seafood dishes in this establishment which is patronized by the Santa Cruz elite.

MESÓN LOS MONJES c/ Marina, 7.
•1200-1600 & 2000-2400. •Moderate.
Meat and fish dishes in Basque style, including a fine cod in squid sauce.

LOS TRONCOS c/ General Goded, 17.
•1200-1600 & 2000-2330. •Budget-Moderate.
The best place in town to sample typical Canarian cuisine. Specialities of the house include fish soup, cress soup and meat dishes.

LA LANGOSTERA San Andrés, 8 km north-east of Santa Cruz.
•1200-2300. Bus, taxi from c/ Marina. •Budget-Moderate.
You'll receive a warm welcome in this family-run fish restaurant offering excellent value, with specialities such as salted sea bream.

DA GIGI Rambla del General Franco, 27.
•1200-1600 & 1900-2400. •Budget.
Tasty homemade pizzas, with rapid but pleasant service.

LA TASCA DEL ENTRENTE c/ Dr Naveiras.
•1300-1600 & 1900-0100. •Budget.
A tiny taperia *offering snacks to the local business people. Try the chips mixed with beef, tortilla, tomato and garlic salad, and the local wine.*

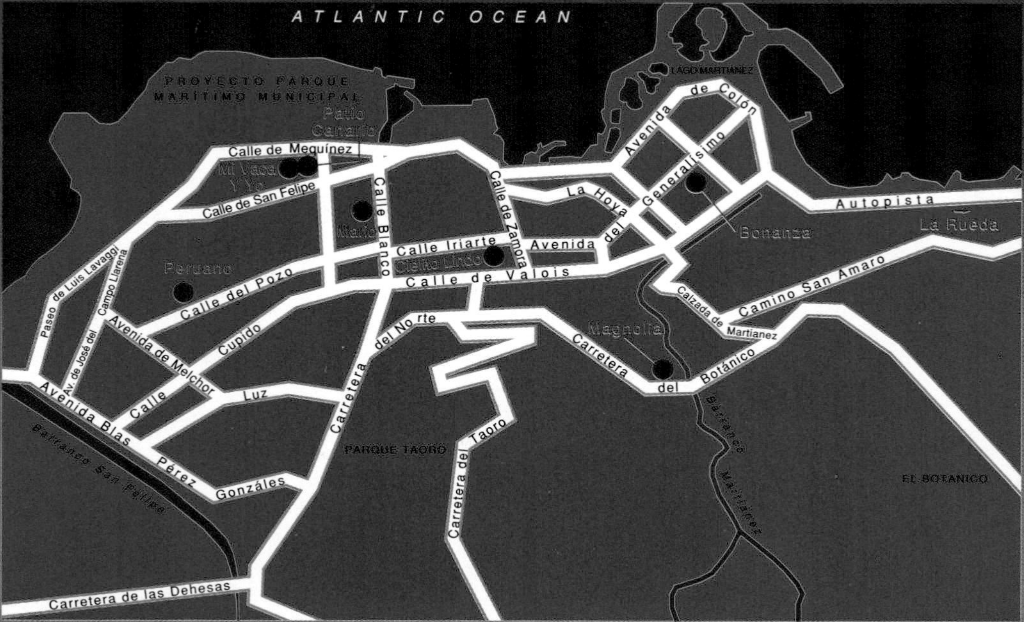
ATLANTIC OCEAN
PROYECTO PARQUE
MARÍTIMO MUNICIPAL
Patio Canario
LAGO MARTIANEZ
Avenida de Colón
Generalísimo
Autopista
La Rueda
Bonanza
Calle de Mequínez
Mi Vaca Y Yo
Calle de San Felipe
Calle Blanco
Calle de Zamora
La Hoya
Avenida del Generalísimo
Calle Iriarte
Avenida
Cielito Lindo
Calle de Valois
Peruano
Calle del Pozo
Paseo de Luis Lavaggi
Campo Llarena
Av. de José del
Avenida de Melchor
Cupido
Calle Luz
Avenida Blas
Pérez Gonzáles
Barranco San Felipe
Carretera del Norte
Carretera del Taoro
PARQUE TAORO
Magnolia
Carretera del Botánico
Calzada de Martianez
Camino San Amaro
Barranco Martianez
EL BOTANICO
Carretera de las Dehesas

Puerto de la Cruz

MARIO Edfo Rincondel Puerto, Pza del Charco.
•1200-1530 & 1900-2400 Tues.-Sun. •Moderate.
Small fish restaurant with wooden decor and fishing nets. Two of the tables are set in a genuine fishing boat. Try their paella, and the fish soup.

MAGNOLIA Ctra del Botánico, 5.
•1900-2400. •Expensive.
Cordon bleu status - one of the best restaurants in town. Excellent Catalan and international dishes.

MI VACA Y YO Cruz Verde, 3.
•1830-2400. •Expensive.
Tropical setting in which to enjoy excellent international cuisine worth the high prices. Try their lobster and wines.

PATIO CANARIO Cruz Verde, 4.
•1300-2400 Wed.-Mon. •Budget-Moderate.
This restaurant serves a wide variety of both regional and international cuisine, including delicious fish brochettes. Cheerful, typically Canarian decor.

LA RUEDA Ctra General del Norte, Sauzal.
•1200-1600 & 1900-2400 Thurs.-Tues. •Moderate.
A family establishment where you can enjoy specialities of fresh barbecued meat and local mushrooms in a pleasant rustic atmosphere.

CIELITO LINDO corner of c/ Esquivel and c/ Virtud.
•1200-1600 & 1900-2400 Mon.-Sat. •Budget-Moderate.
Beautiful painted walls with ornate chairs and candles. Mexican specialities.

PERUANO Apertados San Miguel, c/ del Pozo.
•1200-1600 & 1830-2300. •Budget-Moderate.
Fine Peruvian cuisine and a favourite with the locals.

BONANZA Edfo Avenida, Av del Generalísimo.
•1130-1600 & 1800-2400. •Budget.
English steak house with a good choice and impeccable service.

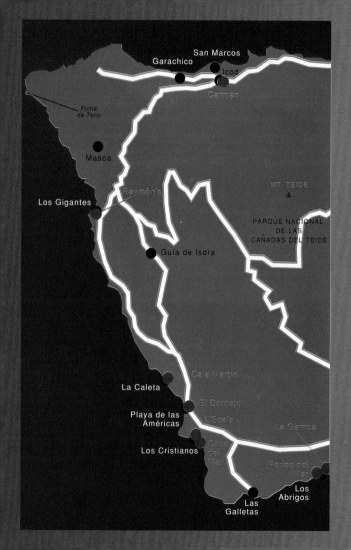

CALA MARÍN La Caleta, near Adeje.
•1200-1600 & 1930-2400. •Moderate.
Delicious seafood, lobster and fresh fish, depending on the day's catch.
Live music and Canarian show at night.

L'SCALA c/ La Paloma 7, Los Cristianos.
•1200-1530 & 1800-2300. •Moderate.
Stone-built restaurant whose specialities include steaks and suckling pig.

CASA DEL MAR Los Cristianos.
•1200-2300 Tues.-Sun. •Moderate.
Distinctively shaped restaurant with a nice view, serving fresh seafood.

LA GAMBA c/ La Marina, Los Abrigos.
•1200-2300 Tues.-Sun. •Moderate.
Good location with a terrace overlooking the port of Los Abrigos.
Simple, but excellent value. Try the paella *or seafood soup.*

PERLAS DEL MAR c/ La Marina, Los Abrigos.
•1100-2300. •Budget-Moderate.
Another popular terrace restaurant where you can select your own fish.

CARMEN c/ Hércules 2, Icod de los Vinos.
•1200-2300 Thurs.-Tues. •Budget.
In a beautiful Canarian house, this restaurant offers various regional tapas
(see **Food**) *and dishes at extremely reasonable prices. See* **EXCURSION 1**.

RAYMÓN'S Av Marítima, Puerto de Santiago.
•1200-1600 & 1930-2300. •Budget.
Terrace restaurant with attractive blue and white decor, and offering a warm
welcome. Raymón's salad, the steaks and the rosé wine are recommended.

EL DORNAJO Av Litoral, Playa de las Américas.
•1300-1600 & 1900-2300. •Budget-Moderate.
The owner is also the chef of this successful Canarian style restaurant.
Good reputation for its grilled meat and selection of fish and seafood.

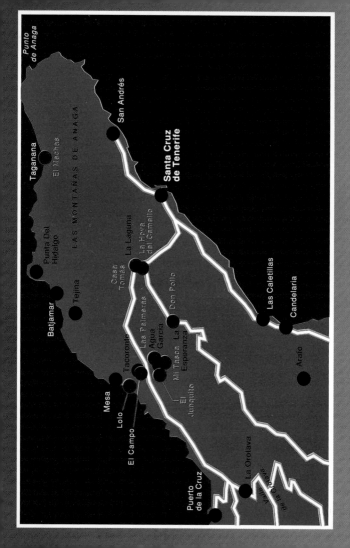

North

EL CAMPO Ctra General del Norte 342, Tacoronte.
•1200-2400 Mon.-Sat., 1200-1500 Sun. •Moderate.
A charming family establishment specializing in grilled meats.

LAS PALMERAS Camino Real 252, Agua García.
•1200-1600 & 1930-2300. •Budget-Moderate.
Grills and fish served on wooden platters, and a variety of tapas (see **Food**).

MI TASCA Camino Real 108, Agua García.
•1100-2400/0100. •Budget-Moderate.
Good standard of food and unusual specialities such as tripe.

EL JUNQUITO Ctra de Agua García 209, Tacoronte.
•1200-2300. Closed Wed. and Sun. evenings. •Budget.
Friendly atmosphere in this rustic Canarian restaurant serving grilled dishes.

CASA TOMÁS Camino del Portezuelo, La Laguna.
•1200-2315. Tues.-Sun. •Budget.
Excellent value typical Canarian home cooking.

LA HOYA DEL CAMELLO Ctra General 118, La Laguna.
•1300-1600 & 1900-2300 Tues.-Sun. •Budget-Moderate.
International and Spanish cuisine, both meat and fish, with friendly service.

DON POLLO El Calverio 73, La Esperanza.
•1200-1600 & 1900-2300. •Budget.
Almost entirely barbecued chicken dishes. Cosy, rustic atmosphere.

EL MECHAS Playa de Taganana, 21 km north of Santa Cruz.
•1100-2300. Bus from c/ Marina, Santa Cruz. •Budget.
A tiny terraced restaurant on the beach, simple and unpretentious.

LOLO El Pris, Tacoronte.
•1200-1600 & 2000-2400 Tues.-Sun. •Budget-Moderate.
Canarian specialities including baked potatoes, mojo picón *and* mojo
verde *(see* **Food**). *Friendly service and modern decor.*

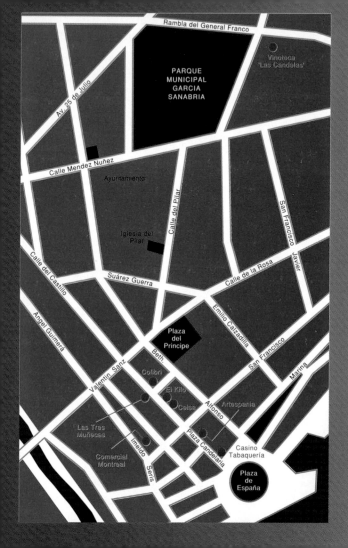

Santa Cruz

ARTESPANIA Pza de la Candelaria, 8.
- 0900-1300 & 1600-1930 Mon.-Fri., 0900-1300 Sat.
State-subsidized craft shop selling a range of inexpensive local pottery, wood carvings, jewellery and paintings.

LAS TRES MUÑECAS c/ Castillo, 15.
- 0930-1300 & 1600-2000 Mon.-Fri., 0930-1300 Sat.
Large and crowded material shop selling silks and haberdashery. Of special interest at carnival time in February and March (see **Events***).*

EL KILO c/ Castillo, 10.
- 0900-1300 & 1600-2000 Mon.-Fri., 0900-1300 Sat.
Another material shop, with a good range of seconds in sheets and towels.

COMERCIAL MONTREAL c/ Dr Allart, 27.
- 0930-1300 & 1630-2000.
Good for Chinese silks and bargains in nightdresses, blouses and kimonos.

VINOTECA LAS CANDELAS Rambla del General Franco, 114.
- 0930-1300 & 1700-2000 Mon.-Fri., 0930-1300 Sat.
Tastefully arranged wine shop with a wide selection from all over the world as well as Spanish and local wines. Friendly and helpful staff.

COLIBRI c/ Castillo, 20; c/ Bethencourt Alfonso, 6.
- 0930-1300 &1630-2000 Mon.-Fri., 0930-1300 Sat.
Silk, wool and leather clothing and accessories designed in-house, much of it exported to Paris and Madrid by the German proprietress.

CASINO TABAQUERÍA c/ de la Marina, 1.
- 0930-2000 Mon.-Fri., 0930-1300 Sat.
Fine tobacconists where you'll also find liqueurs, souvenirs and postcards.

CELSA c/ Castillo, 8.
- 0915-1300 & 1600-1830 Mon.-Fri., 0915-1300 Sat.
A particularly good range of embroidery in both Canarian and oriental styles. Some craftwork, ceramics and precious stones on sale in basement.

ATLANTIC OCEAN

EL BOTANICO

Autopista

Avenida de Colón

Camino San Amaro

Calzada de Martínez

Carretera del Botánico

Barranco Martínez

Calle Generalísimo

Gómez

Casa de la
Real Aduana

Salon
De Paris

Aloha

La Hoya Jep

Poulus

Peletería

Avenida

Calle de Zamora

Calle Iriarte

Casa Iriarte

Calle de Valois

Peletería
Tenerife

Carretera del Toro

Calle Blanco

Carretera Norte

PARQUE TAORO

Carretera del Toro

PROYECTO PARQUE
MARÍTIMO MUNICIPAL

Calle de Mequinez

Calle de San Felipe

Mama Mia

Calle del Pozo

Cupido

Avenida de Melchor

Luz

Calle

Gonzáles

Carretera de las Dehesas

Paseo de Luis Lavaggi

Campo Llarena

Av. de José del

Avenida Blas Pérez

BARRANCO SAN FELIPE

SALÓN DE PARIS c/ Quintana, 13.
•0900-1300 & 1600-2000 Mon.-Fri., 0900-1300 Sat.
Exotic collection of classic furs, with garments from all over the world.

PELETERIA TENERIFE c/ Quintana, 3.
•0900-1300 & 1700-2000 Mon.-Fri., 0900-1300 Sat.
Locally manufactured furs and leathers made to measure or off the peg.

CASA DE LA REAL ADUANA c/ Las Lonjas, 1.
•0930-1300 & 1600-1900 Mon.-Fri., 0930-1300 Sat.
Gifts of embroidery, gold and silverware. See **WALK 3, WHAT TO SEE 3**.

CASA IRIARTE c/ San Juan, 21.
•0900-1300 & 1600-1900 Mon.-Fri., 0900-1300 Sat.
Crafts centre with huge variety of goods. See **WALK 3, WHAT TO SEE 3**.

RELOTERRA Av del Generalisimo, 16.
•1000-1300 & 1600-2000 Mon.-Fri., 1000-1300 Sat.
Jewellery fashioned locally from imported stones.

POULUS c/ Enrique Talg, 2.
•1000-1300 & 1600-2000 Mon.-Fri., 1000-1300 Sat.
Choice of jewellery from classical and expensive to affordable local designs.

GÓMEZ BAEZA c/ San Juan, 10.
•0900-1300 & 1600-2000 Mon.-Fri., 0900-1300 Sat.
The biggest department store in town, with household goods, clothes and furnishings displayed over six floors.

ALOHA c/ Santo Domingo, 12.
•0900-1300 & 1600-2000 Mon.-Fri., 0900-1300 Sat.
Beachwear and sports equipment, including surfboards.

MAMA MÍA c/ San Felipe, 13.
•0900-1300 & 1630-2000 Mon.-Fri., 0900-1300 Sat.
Local and international toys, with a selection of pushchairs for hire.

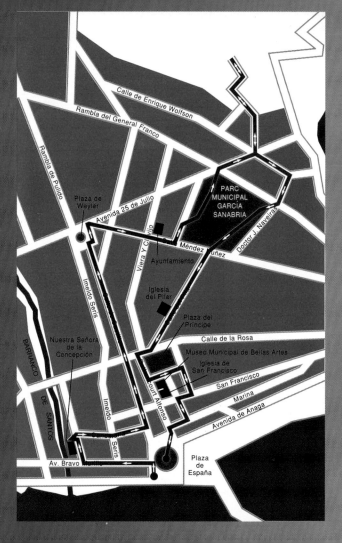

Santa Cruz

2-3 hr

Start from the small tourist office by the side of the Palacio Insular on Plaza de España. Notice the tall obelisk in front of you, the Monumento de los Caídos, in memoriam to those killed in the Spanish Civil War. The view from the top is splendid, but unfortunately the monument is rarely open. On the left is the main entrance to the Palacio Insular, the Canary Islands' administrative offices, where you can see a model of Tenerife. Turn left down the side of the building into Avenida Bravo Murillo and the first door on your left is the entrance to the Museo Arqueológico. See **WHAT TO SEE 1**.

Continue along the avenue and to the right you'll see the modest, whitewashed exterior of the church, Nuestra Señora de la Concepción (see **WHAT TO SEE 1, A-Z**), with its sedate and imposing bell-tower. The entrance to the church is on the Calle del Puente del Cabo. On the Plaza de la Iglesia are what remains of the original city buildings - now undergoing renovation, and quite charming with their wooden balconies in the colonial style.

Outside the church, turn right and head along the Calle Candelaria. Just before you cross the Calle Imelda Seris, you see the Bar Colonial tucked away on a corner to your right. It's worth stopping to admire its interesting curios (see **NIGHTLIFE 1**). Further along you pass the large department store, Maya, before going straight on to the Plaza de la Candelaria. Of architectural interest is the renovated building, now used by the Banco Español de Crédito, known as the Palacio de Carta. See **WHAT TO SEE 1, A-Z**.

Walk up the pedestrian precinct of Calle del Castillo at the top of the square, and browse through its many shops (see **SHOPPING 1**). At the far end is Plaza de Weyler with its pretty marble fountain and overlooked by the impressive building of the Canary Islands Military Headquarters. Turn first right at the far end of the square along Calle Méndez Núñez. This contains the Civil Government buildings on your left and the handsome facade of the *Ayuntamiento* (Town Hall) next to it on the corner. Continue along towards the Parque García Sanabria (see **WHAT TO SEE 1**) where you can relax in the leafy shade of the tropical plants and have a refreshing cool drink.

For the energetic there is a pleasant walk up Avenida 25 de Julio on the opposite side of Rambla del General Franco to the north of the park. Bear left up the narrow, steep road of Calle Fernando Barajas Vilches and climb out of town through the desirable residential area. A 20-30 minute walk will reward you with a splendid view over the city and port. On the way back down turn sharp left into Calle del Enrique Wolfson to admire the beautiful colonial-style town houses and their pastel colours. Turn right into Calle Dr J. Naveiras which will return you to the front entrance of the park.

Head along Calle del Pilar and admire the chic clothes and shoe boutiques. On your right is the Iglesia del Pilar (see **WHAT TO SEE 1**) - an undistinguished facade, but interesting inside. Calle del Pilar takes you past the large store Galerías Preciados and leads on to the side of Plaza del Príncipe. On the opposite side of the square is the Museo Municipal de Bellas Artes (see **WHAT TO SEE 1**) in Calle José Murphy. To the back of the museum is the Iglesia de San Francisco (see **WHAT TO SEE 1**) on the square of the same name. Turn left along Calle Hervas and Calle Villalba and you return to Plaza de España.

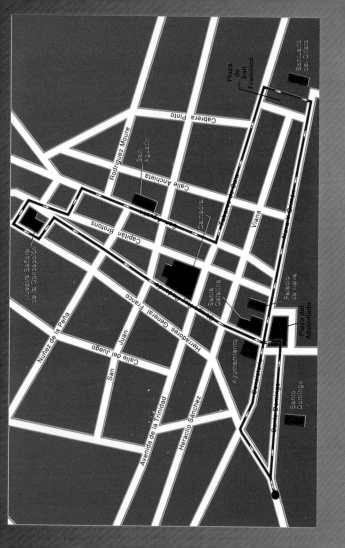

WALK 2

La Laguna

2-3hr

Starting from the terminus of the Santa Cruz bus on Calvo Sotelo, cross over Plaza San Cristóbal and make the gentle ascent of Calle Santo Domingo. On your right is the monastery of Santo Domingo (see **WHAT TO SEE 2**), notable for its Plateresque style of architecture (16th/17thC) and ancient dragon tree (see **Drago**) in the gardens.

Continue up the street to the Plaza del Adelantado, an exceptionally beautiful square bordered by buildings of historical interest. The most striking of these is the Registry Office, with its magnificent carved wooden balcony, so typical of the architecture of the Canary Islands. Next to it stands the market, and diagonally across the shady square stands the 17thC facade of the Palacio de Nava, of pure Baroque style and stately elegance. Next to it is the 16th/17thC monastery of Santa Catalina, and to the left of the monastery on the opposite side of the road is the recently restored *Ayuntamiento* (Town Hall), a fine example of 19thC Canarian architecture (see **WHAT TO SEE 2**). The entrance is on Calle Obispo Rey Redondo which leads off the square, and the interior contains frescoes which depict the history of the island.

Next continue along Calle Obispo Rey Redondo, known by the locals as *La Carrera* (The Street), and glance down its side streets at some of the handsome buildings for which La Laguna is justly renowned. The third turning on the right opens out into Plaza Fray Albino on which stands La Laguna Cathedral (see **WHAT TO SEE 2**, **A-Z**). The setting in the square is tranquility itself as the townsfolk relax on benches and watch the world go by. The Neoclassical facade is by Ventura Rodríguez, and dates from the late 19thC. The twin bell-towers are a landmark. Inside, admire the ornate extravagance of the furnishings and decor.

Continue along Calle Obispo Rey Redondo towards the six-tiered square brick tower of the Iglesia de Nuestra Señora de la Concepción (see **WHAT TO SEE 2**, **A-Z**), visible at the end of the street. The main entrance is on the left, on Plaza Dr Oliviera. This is La Laguna's oldest church, and surely its most beautiful. It contains fine timber carvings on the ceiling and pulpit.

Return to the front of the church on Plaza de la Concepción and take the left hand fork along Calle Capitán Brotons. Turn first left down

Ascanio y Nieves into Calle San Agustín. On the left is the solemn facade of the 17thC church of San Agustín (see **WHAT TO SEE 2**), all that remains after the interior was destroyed by fire at the beginning of the century. Visit the beautiful cloister of the former monastery, which is to the left of the church.

Back outside, turn left and then take the second turning on the left, Calle Tabares de Cala, which leads on to the impressive, open square of Plaza de San Francisco. Diagonally opposite and a little set back from the square is the Santuario del Cristo (see **WHAT TO SEE 2**), housing the 15thC statue of Santísimo Cristo de la Laguna. See **A-Z**.

To return to the bus terminal, take Calle Nava y Grimón, which leads to Plaza del Adelantado, and continue along Calle Consistorio, taking you back to Plaza San Cristóbal.

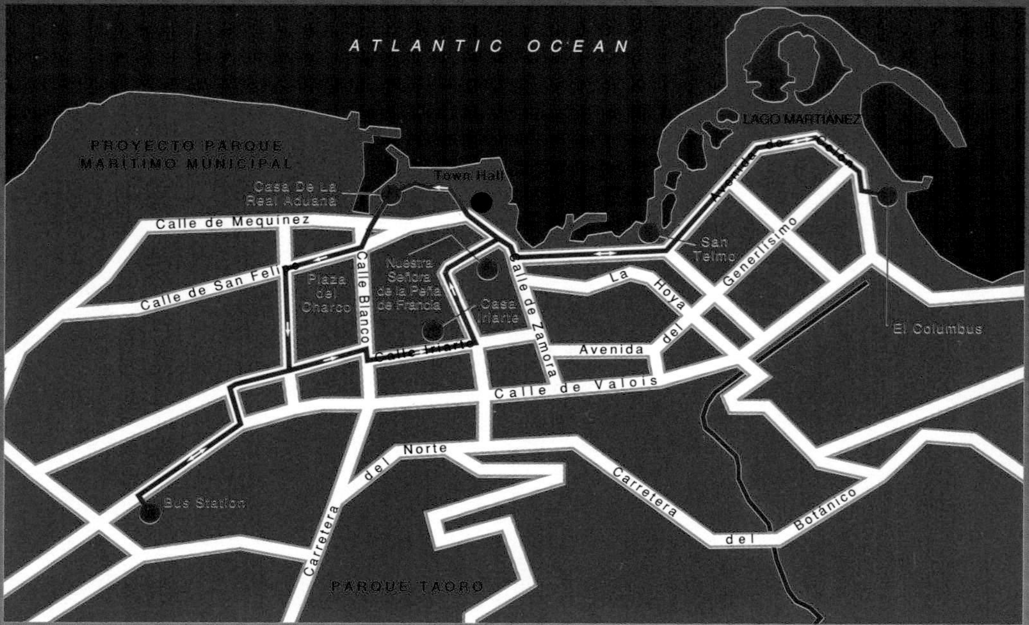
ATLANTIC OCEAN
PROYECTO PARQUE
MARITIMO MUNICIPAL
LAGO MARTIÁNEZ
Casa De La
Real Aduana
Town Hall
Calle de Mequinez
Calle de San Felipe
Plaza
del
Charco
Calle Blanco
Nuestra
Señora
de la Peña
de Francia
Casa
Iriarte
Calle Iriarte
Calle de Zamora
Avenida de Colón
San
Telmo
La Hoya
Generlisimo
Avenida del
Calle de Valois
El Columbus
Carretera del Norte
Carretera del Botánico
Bus Station
PARQUE TAORO

Puerto de la Cruz

2-3hr

From the bus station on Calle del Pozo take Calle Dr Ingram, a street of many shops and restaurants, which leads into Calle Iriarte. This has fine examples of 18thC Canarian architecture, amongst the best of which is the Palacio Ventosa, set in a small square on your right. It is an elegant stone and wood structure which now houses a seminary. Opposite is the Casa Iriarte (see **SHOPPING 2, WHAT TO SEE 3**), the birthplace of the author, Tomás de Iriarte (1750-1791), now containing many craft shops. Continue up the picturesque flight of steps on Calle Iriarte and turn left into Calle Cologan, leading to the Plaza de la Peña de Francia. The square is bordered by the post office and tourist office. The bust in the centre is of Agustín de Bethencourt y Molina (1758-1824), a locally born inventor and engineer. Inside the Iglesia de Nuestra Señora de la Peña de Francia (see **WHAT TO SEE 3**), which backs onto the square, are some beautiful wooden figurines and a fine Baroque altarpiece.

From the church, turn right and take the Calle de San Telmo along the seafront. You soon come to the Capilla San Telmo, a fishermen's chapel built in 1626. On the left is the Lago de Martiánez complex. If you wish, continue along Avenida de Colón until you reach El Columbus on the left (see **NIGHTLIFE 2**). Here you could sample some of their delicious pastries while enjoying an unimpeded view of the sea.

Alternatively, retrace your steps through the craft and souvenir stalls of Calle de San Telmo. At the end of the promenade a popular pastime is to watch the waves break spectacularly against the rocks below (see **BEACHES 2**). From here, bear right down Calle de Santo Domingo to enter the older part of town. At the bottom, turn right onto Calle Las Lonjas. At the foot of this picturesque cobbled street is the Casa de la Real Aduana (see **SHOPPING 3, WHAT TO SEE 3**).

The charming fishing port, Puerto Pesquero, is a small stretch of sand protected by two breakwaters and harbouring small fishing boats which add a touch of colour to the scene. Once it served as a port for La Orotava and handled 80% of the island's trade. Bear left towards the Plaza del Charco (see **WHAT TO SEE 3**), bordered by 18thC buildings. From here, wander through the charming streets of the old town, with its boutiques and restaurants, bearing west to return to the bus station.

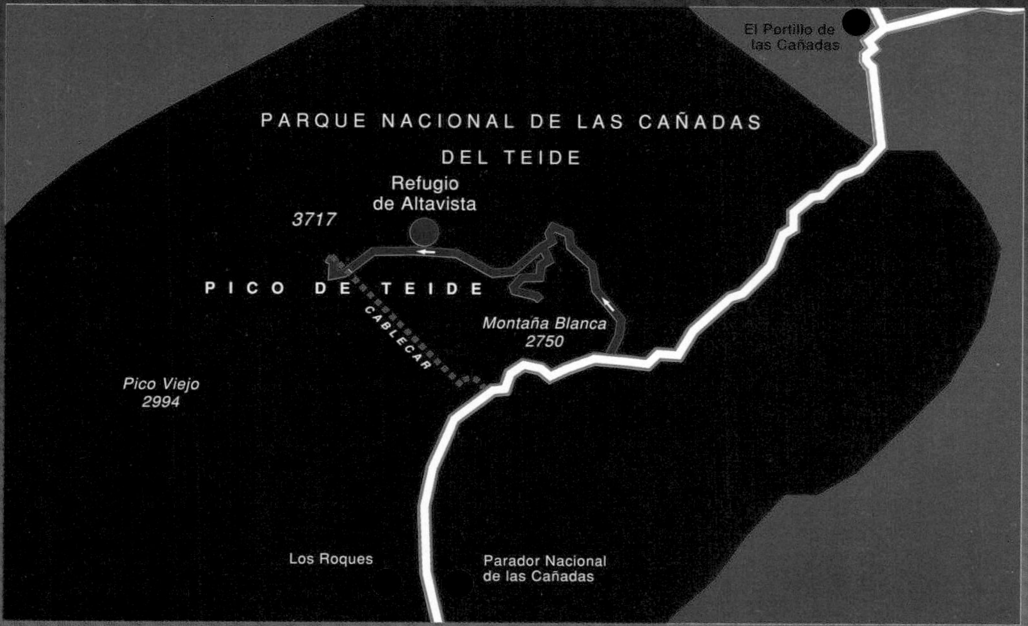
El Portillo de las Cañadas
PARQUE NACIONAL DE LAS CAÑADAS DEL TEIDE
Refugio de Altavista
3717
PICO DE TEIDE
CABLECAR
Montaña Blanca 2750
Pico Viejo 2994
Los Roques
Parador Nacional de las Cañadas

Mount Teide

3-4hr

The ascent of Mount Teide (see **EXCURSION 2,A-Z**) via Montaña Blanca
is strenuous in places, so bring proper climbing boots, warm clothing
and a supply of water. The road doesn't end until deceptively high up
into the mountains, so it is easy to forget that you are climbing at altitudes of 2300-3700 m. The cable car will not operate on windy days,
so check the weather prospects before setting out. For information,
consult the Centro de Visitantes at El Portillo.
Take Bus 348 (0830 Wed.-Sun., from Puerto de la Cruz) and alight at
the Montaña Blanca stop. A signpost gives an outline of the network of
paths. The ascent begins with a pleasant climb along a gravel path with
views back to Las Cañadas (see **A-Z**) and of the mountains to the north
and cliffs on the north-east coast. After 60-70 minutes turn right at the
signpost for the Refugio de Altavista. The path becomes rougher and
the ascent steeper as it traverses the terrain above the floor of the crater
of Las Cañadas. After 60 minutes or so of hard climbing over pitted,
sandy-coloured stone and pebbles, you reach the mountain refuge
(accommodation bookings from tourist office). Continue along the path
behind the refuge through a landscape littered with large boulders. On
the right (after 10-15 min) is a path leading to the Cueva del Hielo, with
its ice stalactites. Back on the original path, the slope levels out and
you come to a fork where you keep straight on. Shortly afterwards
you'll see the cable car terminus below on the left. Turn right when you
get to the main path up to the summit. Cracks in the ground emit steam
and the air is filled with the odour of sulphur. You arrive at the summit
(45-60 min), which consists of a small crater. To the south west you'll
see Pico Viejo in gentle hues of mauve and brown, and below you is
the floor of Las Cañadas crater, revealing the stark beauty of its barren
landscape. At 3717 m, you're above the clouds and flight paths. On a
clear day, the view embraces Gomera, La Palma, Hierro and Gran
Canaria (see **ISLANDS, A-Z**). When you've had enough of the majestic
views and buffeting of the wind, make the 20 minute descent towards
the cable car terminus (last descent 1600). Here you can have a drink
while you wait your turn. The descent takes 8 minutes and you can
catch the same bus (348) back to Puerto de la Cruz.

Avenida General Mora

Calle General Goded

Avenida de la Asunción

Rambla del General Franco

Calle Robayna

Calle Ramón Y Cajal

Rambla de Pulido

Plaza de Toros

Parque García Sanabria

Avenida 25 de Julio

Viera Y Clavijo

Calle Galcerán

Calle Méndez Nuñez

Avenida la Salle

Calle de San Sebastián

Imeldo Seris

Calle del Pilar

Calle del Pilar

Iglesia del Pilar

Museo Municipal de Bellas Artes

Calle de la Rosa

Nuestra Señora de la Concepción

Calle del Castillo

Bethencourt Alfonso

Plaza del Príncipe

Iglesia de San Francisco

Puente Serrador

Calle San Francisco

Avenida Cuba Marina

Nuestra Señora de África

Imeldo Seris

Cruz Verde

Avenida de Anaga

Castillo de Paso Alto

Avenida Tres de Mayo

Avenida Bravo Murillo

Plaza de España

Palacio de Carta

José Antonio Primo de Rivera

Museo Arqueológico

Calle de

Barranco

MUSEO MUNICIPAL DE BELLAS ARTES c/ José Murphy, 4.
• 1000-2000 Mon.-Fri.
Fine collection of paintings and sculpture. Displays the work of Canarian artists as well as Brueghel, Ribera, Jordaens, Van Loo, etc. See **WALK 1**.

MUSEO ARQUEOLÓGICO Palacio Insular, c/ Bravo Murillo.
• 0900-1300 & 1600-1800 Mon.-Fri., 0900-1300 Sat. • 200ptas.
Guanche (see **A-Z**) *artefacts, ceramics, mummies, etc. See* **WALK 1**.

IGLESIA DE SAN FRANCISCO Pza de San Francisco.
• According to Masses.
Late 17thC Franciscan chapel featuring handsome Baroque sculptures.

IGLESIA DEL PILAR c/ del Pilar.
• According to Masses.
18thC church with a fine painted ceiling. See **WALK 1**.

PALACIO DE CARTA Pza de la Candelaria, 8.
• 0900-1400 Mon.-Fri.
Splendid Canarian interior patio with tropical plants. See **WALK 1**, **A-Z**.

CASTILLO DE PASO ALTO Av Anaga.
• For opening check at tourist office. Taxi, Bus from Pza de España.
Castle converted to a military museum. See **Nelson, Horatio**.

NUESTRA SEÑORA DE ÁFRICA c/ San Sebastián.
• 0630-1300 Mon.-Sat.
The city's main market, housed in an enormous renovated building.

PARQUE GARCÍA SANABRIA West of city, near c/ del Pilar.
• Open at all times.
The municipal park, a jumble of rare tropical plants. See **WALK 1**.

NUESTRA SEÑORA DE LA CONCEPCIÓN Pza de la Iglesia.
• 0730-1000, 1230-1300 & 1700-2030.
18thC Baroque church with magnificent sculpted altar. See **WALK 1**, **A-Z**.

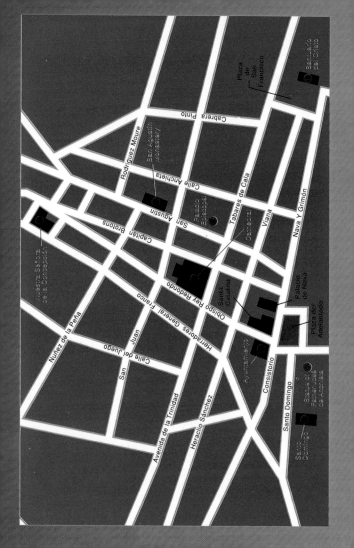

LA LAGUNA CATHEDRAL Pza de la Catedral.

•0800-1000, 1700-2030, and according to Masses.
18thC Neoclassical facade housing many treasures. See WALK 2, A-Z.

NUESTRA SEÑORA DE LA CONCEPCIÓN

Pza de la Concepción.
•According to masses.
Founded in 1497 and the oldest of Tenerife's churches. See WALK 2, A-Z.

AYUNTAMIENTO (TOWN HALL) Pza del Adelantado.

•0900-1300.
19thC building beautifully restored in typical Canarian style. See WALK 2.

SANTO DOMINGO Pza de Santo Domingo, 1.

•Opening times from town hall.
See the beautiful dragon tree in the monastery gardens and admire the frescoes housed in this 16th/17thC early Renaissance church. See WALK 2.

SAN AGUSTÍN MONASTERY c/ San Agustín.

•0830-early evening Mon.-Fri., 0830-1300 Sat.
Wander round the beautiful inner cloister of this former 17thC monastery, largely destroyed in a fire at the beginning of the century. See WALK 2.

PALACIO EPISCOPAL c/ San Agustín.

Interior closed to public.
Elegant 17thC Baroque palace built by the Counts of Salazar.

STATUE OF FATHER JOSÉ DE ANCHIETA

Opposite university buildings on roundabout at entrance to town.
A bronze sculpture by Bruno Giggi (1959), donated by the Brazilian government, in honour of this missionary who came from La Laguna.

SANTUARIO DEL CRISTO Pza de San Francisco.

•Opening times from town hall.
One of the most venerated images on the island, the Santísimo Cristo de la Laguna (see A-Z*), is housed in this former Franciscan chapel. See* WALK 2.

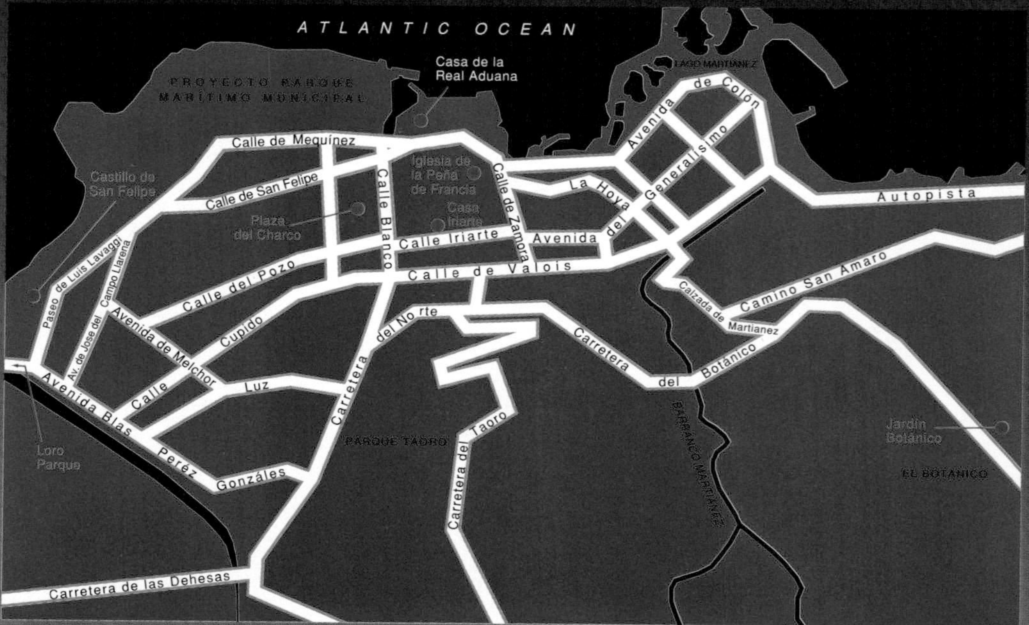
ATLANTIC OCEAN
Casa de la Real Aduana
PROYECTO PARQUE MARÍTIMO MUNICIPAL
LAGO MARTIANEZ
Avenida de Colón
Generalísimo
Autopista
La Hoya
Avenida del
Calle de Mequínez
Iglesia de la Peña de Francia
Casa Iriarte
Castillo de San Felipe
Calle de San Felipe
Plaza del Charco
Calle Blanco
Calle de Zamora
Calle Iriarte
Calle de Valois
Calle del Pozo
Paseo de Luis Lavaggi
Av. de Jose del Campo Llarena
Avenida de Melchor
Cupido
Calle Luz
Avenida Blas Peréz Gonzáles
Carretera del Norte
Calzada de Martianez
Camino San Amaro
Carretera del Botánico
Loro Parque
PARQUE TAORO
Carretera del Taoro
BARRANCO MARTIANEZ
Jardín Botánico
EL BOTÁNICO
Carretera de las Dehesas

IGLESIA DE LA PEÑA DE FRANCIA Pza de la Iglesia.
•Open according to Masses.
Much altered facade but inside are examples of the work of the Canarian artist Luis de la Cruz and the sculptor Luján Pérez. See **WALK 3**.

CASA IRIARTE c/ San Juan.
•0900-1300 & 1600-1900 Mon.-Fri., 0900-1300 Sat.
An 18thC mansion boasting fine carved balconies and a pretty patio. Now houses craft studios, shops, a naval museum and an interesting display of historical photographs of the area. See **SHOPPING 2**, **WALK 3**.

CASTILLO DE SAN FELIPE Paseo de Luis Lavaggi.
Interior closed to public. Free bus from Pl Martiánez.
An 18thC castle of interest for its Spanish colonial-style facade, which displays the coat of arms of Philip IV of Spain. Set in an attractive garden.

PLAZA DEL CHARCO At the foot of c/ Blanco.
The focal point of the town, with imported Indian laurel trees and a children's playground. Stop and watch the world go by. See **WALK 3**.

CASA DE LA REAL ADUANA c/ Lonjas.
•0930-1300 & 1600-1900 Mon.-Fri., 0930-1300 Sat.
The oldest surviving building in Puerto de la Cruz, dating from 1620, and formerly a Customs House. The inner patio now houses craft and souvenir shops. See **SHOPPING 2**, **WALK 3**.

LORO PARQUE c/ San Felipe, Punta Brava.
•0830-1800. Bus from Pl Martiánez. •1225ptas, child 600ptas.
Over 1300 parrots in a beautiful tropical setting with spectacular shows throughout the day. Trained parrots, dolphins and other animals.

JARDÍN BOTÁNICO Ctra del Botánico.
•0900-1900 summer, 0900-1800 winter. •100ptas.
A marvellous display of plants, both indigenous to the Canaries and from all over the world. Created in the late 18thC, the gardens demonstrate the benefits of the local climate. See **A-Z**.

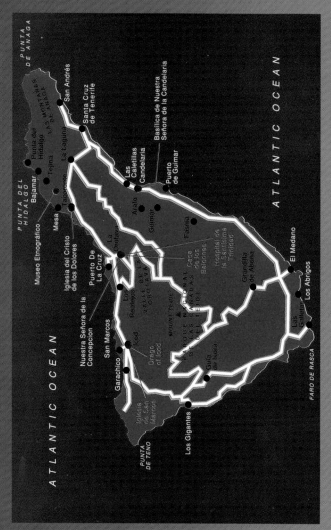

BASÍLICA DE NUESTRA SEÑORA DE LA CANDELARIA
Av Litoral, Candelaria.
•0730-1300 & 1500-2030 (winter till 1930), and according to Masses.
Built near the seafront in 1958 to house the replica of the famous Virgen de la Candelaria. *See* **Candelaria**, **Nuestra Señora de la Candelaria**.

DRAGO OF ICOD c/ Hércules, Icod de los Vinos.
Magnificent dragon tree, perhaps 3000 years old. See EXCURSION 1, **A-Z**.

NUESTRA SEÑORA DE LA CONCEPCIÓN
Pza Casanas, La Orotava.
•According to Masses.
Baroque facade housing a splendid high altarpiece. See EXCURSION 1, **A-Z**.

CASA DE LOS BALCONES c/ San Francisco, La Orotava.
•0900-1300 & 1600-1930 Mon.-Fri., 0900-1300 Sat.
17thC building with beautiful carved wooden balconies. Visit the patio and watch girls in national costume doing embroidery work. See EXCURSION 1.

HOSPITAL DE LA SANTÍSIMA TRINIDAD
Pza San Francisco, La Orotava.
•1600-1730 (also 1030-1200 Sun. and hols).
Former monastery with a fine view of the Orotava valley. See EXCURSION 1.

IGLESIA DEL CRISTO DE LOS DOLORES
Pza de San Agustín, Tacoronte.
•According to Masses.
Houses a revered 17thC statue of Christ. See EXCURSION 3, **A-Z**.

MUSEO ETNOGRÁFICO Ctra Tacoronte, Valle Guerra.
•1000-1300 & 1600-1900. •200ptas (children/students half price).
Pleasing display of crafts, tools and 'life as it used to be'. See EXCURSION 3.

IGLESIA DE SAN MARCOS Pza de la Iglesia, Icod de los Vinos.
•According to Masses.
Renaissance-style church with a painted wooden ceiling. See EXCURSION 1.

FABRICA D

PLAYA DE

GON

Accidents and Breakdowns: If you are involved in a motoring accident, follow normal procedure by exchanging insurance details, names and addresses with the other party. Try to establish witnesses' details also. If someone is injured call the police (see **Emergencies**). If you are driving your own car you will need a surety bond from your insurance company to exempt you from having to spend time in police custody while awaiting the outcome of any enquiry.

In cases of breakdown, the Real Automóvil Club de Tenerife (the local equivalent of the RAC) offers reciprocal membership to drivers who subscribe to a club in their own country. Their office is on Avenida Anaga, Santa Cruz, tel: 27.07.16.

If you are driving a hired car, instructions on what to do in case of accident and breakdown should be printed on your contract.

See **Garages**.

Accommodation: In the high season it is essential to book a hotel prior to arrival as a large amount of the available accommodation consists of hotels which deal with travel firms offering package holidays. The same classification of hotels operates as on the mainland.

Paradores are luxurious, state-owned hotels. There is one on Tenerife, the Parador Nacional Las Cañadas del Teide, rated two-star. Although of moderate size, it has facilities such as swimming pool, bar and tennis court. Tel: 33.23.04. See **EXCURSION 2**.

Hotels range from five-star (luxurious) to one-star (comfortable but basic). Approximate prices for a double room during the high season are 20,000ptas (five-star), 4500ptas (three-star) and 3000ptas (one-star). *Hostales* (HS) are rated on a star system of one to three and generally provide much simpler accommodation. A *fonda* (inn) is often good value though usually based only in villages. *Pensiones* cater for the bed and breakfast market and are also rated on a one- to three-star scale. On booking in you will be asked for your passport which will be returned to you the following morning.

Self-catering, villa-style accommodation is also very popular and needs to be arranged prior to arrival. Time-share apartments and villas are also very much on the increase.

See also **Camping**.

Airports: Two airports serve Tenerife. The main international airport is at Reina Sofía to the south of the island, 65 km from Santa Cruz, tel: 77.00.50. It handles regular flights to the mainland by several leading airlines and caters for numerous charter flights. You will also find the usual facilities including car hire agencies, a post office, a *bureau de change*, wheelchair facilities, information services, a self-service restaurant and a bookshop. Bus and taxi services operate between the airport and the main towns. A green TITSA bus to Santa Cruz costs 450ptas and operates in conjunction with scheduled Air Iberia flights. A taxi to Santa Cruz will cost 4000-4500ptas.

The other airport is at Los Rodeos, near La Laguna. It handles relatively inexpensive inter-island flights by Air Iberia. Tel: 25.97.40. Bus services are available and a taxi to Santa Cruz will cost around 1000ptas.

Anaga Mountains: A mountain range in the north-eastern corner of Tenerife, peaking at over 1000 m. The steep slopes and deep gullies are spectacular, and the lower hillsides lush with vegetation, as in the Las Mercedes forest. Of the numerous viewpoints, Pico del Inglés is per-

haps the best. The mountains offer many good walks for the active holi-day-maker and buses to the region leave Santa Cruz from Avenida de Anaga by the Plaza de España. See **EXCURSION 3**.

Babysitters: The best way to find a reliable babysitter is to ask at your hotel. Two or three days notice may be required during the high season and you can expect to pay 500ptas per hr. See **Children**.

Bajamar: 35 km north-east of Puerto de la Cruz. One of the more out-of-the-way tourist resorts to the north-east of the island, set on cliffs beneath the impressive backdrop of the Anaga Mountains (see **A-Z**), and with modern apartments and hotels spreading towards the nearby Punta del Hidalgo. A quiet spot of fishing is a popular pastime on the seafront, where there is also a tiny beach in a protected cove, and sea-water swimming pools. See **EXCURSION 3**.

Banana Plantations: The banana has been vital to the economy of the Canary Islands for more than a hundred years now, having been introduced from Indo-China in the latter part of the 19thC. Recently,

production and marketing difficulties have necessitated government intervention in the form of subsidies. The industry still appears to be in danger and many farmers are turning to other crops. Most of the remaining banana plantations are in the north (see **EXCURSION 3**). The guided tour of the Bananera el Guanche, near La Orotava, gives an interesting insight into the process of banana cultivation.

Banks: They are plentiful in the major towns and offer all the customary services. Their charges for exchanging currency are likely to be lower than the *bureaux de change*.
Banco de Bilbao - Plaza de la Candelaria, Santa Cruz. Tel: 24.46.83.
Banco Exterior de España - La Marina 8, Puerto de la Cruz. Tel: 38.34.52.
See **Opening Times**.

Barranco del Infierno: An immense and beautiful gorge near the town of Adeje in the south-west of Tenerife. It provides a very popular walk which few people will find too strenuous.

Best Buys: Santa Cruz is a free trade port. There are no restrictions on the source of supply of articles, taxes are very low, and there is no VAT. Therefore, an extremely wide range of cheap electrical goods, cameras, watches, perfume, jewellery and spirits is available. Furs are also inexpensive at about 40% less than elsewhere in Europe. Nevertheless, shoppers should be alert, as some apparent bargains may be goods of inferior quality. Local crafts include embroidery and lace, basketwork, pottery, wooden carvings and rugs. Cigars are also good value due to the availability of home-grown tobacco. See **SHOPPING**, **Shopping**.

Bethencourt, Jean de (1359-1425): A Norman nobleman, he set off in 1402 to conquer the Canary Islands, under the orders of King Henry III of Castile. Having captured Lanzarote (see **ISLANDS, A-Z**) he was named 'King of the Canaries' by Henry, and went on to take Fuerteventura and Hierro in 1405 (see **ISLANDS, A-Z**). His attempt to conquer Gran Canaria (see **ISLANDS, A-Z**) the following year failed, and the final conquest was left to Isabella and Ferdinand, in 1483.

Bicycle Hire: Because of Tenerife's mountainous terrain and steep winding roads the hiring of bicycles is fairly uncommon and not really recommended for the casual cyclist.

Bobadilla, Beatriz de (15thC): A significant figure in the history of the Canary Islands. She and her husband, Hernán Peraza the Younger, displayed great cruelty towards the islanders while governing Gomera (see **ISLANDS, EXCURSION 5, A-Z**). Beatriz was forced to retreat

to the safety of the Torre del Conde in San Sebastián following an uprising in 1488 during which Hernán was killed. Following the re-establishment of her authority she entertained the explorer Christopher Columbus (see **A-Z**) during his visits to Gomera and speculation remains that they had an affair. Her powerful position was confirmed by her marriage to Alonso Fernández de Lugo (see **A-Z**) in 1498.

Budget: The cost of living is generally quite moderate in Tenerife, although self-catering holiday-makers should expect some grocery items to cost more than they may be used to.

Breakfast - 500-600ptas.

Lunch - Dish of the day in a restaurant will be approximately 500ptas.

Dinner - 1500-3000ptas.

Wine - 235ptas bottle from supermarket, 500ptas bottle in restaurant.

Soft Drinks - 125ptas per litre.

Discos - 600-800ptas.

Museums - 200ptas.

Buenavista: 35 km west of Puerto de la Cruz. An archetypal small Canarian community, nestling beneath the Teno mountain range. You can sample a real taste of village life here as children play in the tree-lined square beside the town's church, Virgen de los Remedios. A track leads from the village to the westernmost tip of the island at Punta de Teno, going past the Mirador de Don Pompeyo which offers a scenic prospect back to the town. The road from Buenavista to Santiago del Teide is one of the most spectacular on the island as it rises through the Valle del Palmar. See **EXCURSION 1**.

Bullfighting: Occasional bullfights are held in the Plaza de Toros, off Rambla del General Franco in Santa Cruz. They are extensively advertized around town.

Buses: The main bus company on Tenerife is TITSA, tel: 21.56.99 (Santa Cruz) and 38.18.07 (Puerto de la Cruz). It operates an extensive and punctual service through most of the resorts and towns of the island. Buses are air-conditioned and clean. The main bus station in Santa Cruz is on Avenida Tres de Mayo where you can reserve a seat for express services (generally only necessary at weekends when buses are crowded with families). The Puerto de la Cruz bus station is situated on Calle del Pozo.

Cameras and Photography: Cameras are relatively cheap on Tenerife. Films are generally of reasonable quality, and there are plenty of 24-hr developing services. Make allowances for the strong sunlight, especially when taking pictures near whitewashed walls or the sand

and sea. Some museums may allow photography, but it is not permitted near military installations.

Camping: There is an official camp site at Nauta Camping, Cañada Blanca, Arona. Tel: 78.51.18. Basic charges start at 250ptas per person for one night, with additional costs for cars, *etc*. It is well equipped, with a restaurant, a shop, sports facilities and a swimming pool, and is situated not far from the south coast beaches.

Canary Islands: Situated in an area some 100-300 km off the northwest African coast, the seven main islands in the group are (from east to west) Lanzarote, Fuerteventura, Gran Canaria, Tenerife, Gomera, La Palma and Hierro. See **ISLANDS, A-Z**.

The ancient title of the archipelago was the Blessed or Fortunate Islands, but the true origin of the name Canary Islands is still uncertain. Suggestions are that the Romans gave the islands their title after the Latin for dog, *canis*, or that it was named after *canna*, an indigenous plant, or *canora*, a singing bird. The islands are now a major tourist destination for summer and winter sun holidays.

Candelaria: 20 km south-west of Santa Cruz. A small fishing town built on a hillside situated just beneath (but hidden from) the *Autopista del Sur*. In August, pilgrims from all over the Canaries converge on the Basílica de Nuestra Señora de la Candelaria (see **WHAT TO SEE 4**). It is set on an open square with a fountain and artificial waterfall to one side. The square is bordered by pleasant cafés and whitewashed houses with carved balconies. On the seafront, red stone statues of Guanche kings (see **A-Z**) stand with their backs to Candelaria's small pebbly beach. The basilica, a modern church, features frescoes, small rounded stained glass windows, imposing stone arches, and a delightful small wooden carved and painted pulpit. The chief attraction, however, is the statue of Nuestra Señora de la Candelaria (see **A-Z**), glittering in the splendour of her pedestal.

Car Hire: If you are travelling on a package holiday and know the type of car and number of days hire you need, it is usually cheaper to book in advance through your travel firm. There are, however, many agencies in the main resorts and bigger towns, as well as at Reina Sofía (see **Airports**). Local agents are generally cheaper than the international companies, but make sure that the contract you sign is in English and that insurance is included. Minimum age is 23 when paying in cash, or 21 with a credit card. You will need either a national or international driving licence, issued at least one year previously. Prices are around 2300ptas per day for a Fiat Panda and 2500ptas for a Renault 5, but insurance (600-800ptas per day) and a 4% tax are always added to the original quoted prices. See **Driving**.

Chemists: Chemists are easily identified by their distinctive sign of a green cross. Opening hours (see **A-Z**) are the same as for other shops, with late opening determined by a rota system to ensure 24-hr service. Check in the window for the name and address of the nearest after-hours pharmacy.

Children: Children can readily be kept occupied in Tenerife and will enjoy the sea and sand and many of the available excursions. The Canarians love children and they will always be made welcome. There

are several children's playgrounds in Santa Cruz and some child-care
facilities if you wish to do some shopping or sightseeing on your own.
La Guagua Feliz is a converted bus parked by the Plaza del Príncipe,
with trained staff who will look after children aged two to seven years.
Open 1000-1300, 1700-2030; 250ptas per hr.
Caperucita Roja on c/ Enrique Wilson is a fully-equipped nursery for
children from three months to six years of age. There are sleeping and
eating facilities, an outdoor play area, and friendly local staff. Open
0730-1930; 250ptas per hr plus 500ptas for a meal. Tel: 27.60.75.

Climate: The Canary Islands enjoy a temperate climate all year
round, with little seasonal variation. On Tenerife the weather is affected
by the mountains which separate the north and south coasts. The northern coast is often slightly cooler due to the *alisio* wind. In winter the
south-western coastal resorts are more likely to enjoy sunny weather.
Due to the topography of Tenerife it is possible to experience the whole
range of weather conditions when driving round the island, from sun-
drenched beaches to misty woodlands to the snow-capped peak of
Mount Teide (see **EXCURSION 2**, **WALK 4**, **A-Z**).
In Santa Cruz the average temperature in January is 17.5°C (maximum
20.4°C, minimum 14.7°C), and in August 25.2°C (maximum 29.3C,
minimum 21.1C).

Columbus, Christopher (1451-1506): At the beginning of his
expedition that led to the discovery of America in 1492, Columbus
stopped at Las Palmas on Gran Canaria (see **A-Z**) for supplies and
repairs. It was the first of four such visits he was to pay to the Canaries,
giving rise to the rumour that he was in love with the Spanish exile,
Beatriz de Bobadilla (see **A-Z**). The house in which he is said to have
resided can be seen in San Sebastián on Gomera. See **EXCURSION 5**.

Complaints: The same system operates as on the Spanish mainland,
though you are probably less likely to have to resort to the procedure,
given the friendly and hospitable nature of the Canarians. Every hotel
must keep a supply of *hojas de reclamaciones* (complaints forms), and
often simply requesting one is sufficient to achieve results. If not, fill in

the form in 3 copies, one to retain, one for the Tourist Board, and one for the establishment against which the complaint is being made. Such a procedure is treated very seriously and should not be abused. For major complaints involving violence or fraud, go directly to the police (see **A-Z**) or Tourist Office. See **Tourist Information**.

Consulates:
UK - Floor 5, c/ Suárez Guerra 40, Santa Cruz. Tel: 28.68.63.
Republic of Ireland - Floor 6, c/ La Marina 7, Santa Cruz. Tel: 24.56.71.
USA - c/ Alvarez de Lugo 10, Santa Cruz. Tel: 28.69.50.

Conversion Charts:

TEMPERATURE
°C   −30 −25 −20 −15 −10 −5   0   5   10   15   20   25   30   35   40   45
°F   −20 −10   0   10   20   30   40   50   60   70   80   90   100   110

DISTANCE
kms   0   1   2   3   4   5   6   8   10   12   14   16
miles   0   ½   1   1½   2   3   4   5   6   7   8   9   10

WEIGHT
grams   0   100   200   300   400   500   600   700   800   900   1 kg
ounces   0   4   8   12   1 lb   20   24   28   2 lb

Credit Cards: Eurocheques are normally accepted in the larger establishments, as are all major credit cards.
American Express - Puerto de la Cruz. Tel: 38.13.50.
Barclays - Plaza de Weyler 8, Santa Cruz. Tel: 28.52.66.

Crime and Theft: Certain simple precautions can be taken to help

prevent a theft from spoiling your holiday: leave all valuables in the hotel safe; don't carry large amounts of cash around with you; don't take valuables to the beach; leave the car in an official car park which has an attendant; if your room has a balcony, remember to close the windows before going out. If you are robbed, you should inform the hotel at once and they will contact the police. In case of theft in the street, go to the police who will help you make the necessary statement for any insurance claim. If you have financial problems or lose your passport, you should also contact your consulate. See **A-Z**.

Cristo de los Dolores: Housed in the chapel of a former Augustinian monastery in Tacoronte (see **EXCURSION 3, WHAT TO SEE 4**), this 17thC statue was modelled on an engraving by the German artist, Albrecht Dürer (1471-1528). It was brought to the island from Madrid by Thomas Pereida in 1662 and depicts a resurrected Christ clasping the crucifix in his arms. It is a particularly beautiful and original image, and is much revered by the islanders.

Currency: The local unit of currency is the peseta (pta).
Coins - 1, 5, 10, 25, 50, 100, 200, 500ptas.
Notes - 100, 500, 1000, 2000, 5000ptas.
Older coins (with Franco's head on them) and the larger, ornate notes are no longer legal tender.

Customs:

Duty Paid Into:	Cigarettes	or	Cigars	or	Tobacco	Spirits	Wine
E.E.C.	300		75		400 g	1.5 l	5 l
Duty Free Into: U.K.	200		50		250 g	1 l	2 l

Disabled: Provision is made for holiday-makers confined to wheel-chairs in many parts of Tenerife. Reina Sofía (see **Airports**) has facilities for the disabled, and the modern resorts such as Playa de las Américas and Los Cristianos (see **A-Z**) have a number of ramps giving access to restaurants, *etc*. The Centro de Visitantes in El Portillo (see **EXCURSION 2**) also has details of a short 1/2 km signposted walk in the Parque Nacional del Teide (see **A-Z**) for the partially disabled or handicapped.

Doctors: See **Health**.

Drago: The Spanish name for the dragon tree or *Dracaena draco*. On Tenerife there are several specimens of this strange-looking tree which often has a huge trunk, crowned with a thick mass of dagger-like leaves. A survivor from the Tertiary era, it is extremely difficult to grow elsewhere. The blood-red sap was used by the Guanches (see **A-Z**) in medicines and mummifying fluid. The most famous *drago* is at Icod de los Vinos (see **EXCURSION 1**, **WHAT TO SEE 4**), and there are other fine examples at La Laguna (see **WALK 2**) and Tacoronte (see **EXCURSION 3**).

Drinks: Locally-produced drinks include *ron* (white rum), liqueurs made from coffee, orange and bananas, and wines which, although hard to find in tourist areas, offer a pleasant accompaniment to a meal in village inns. Don't be surprised if your wine is served in a soft drink bottle, as this means that it has been drawn straight from the barrel. The most famous wine is *malvasía* or malmsey.

Typical Spanish drinks found on the island include *sangría* (an often potent mixture of wine, orange juice and spirits, made up with fruit), *jerez* or sherry (the two main varieties being *fino* for aperitifs and *oloroso* to accompany desserts), the local brandy or *coñac* (rougher than its French counterpart), and *cerveza* or beer (a popular and cheap drink, both locally-produced and imported from the mainland).

Driving: If you decide to take your own car to Tenerife, you'll need your driving licence (preferably an international driving permit), green card insurance, bail bond (also from your insurance company), and the vehicle registration document. For car hire see **A-Z**. You must wear your seat belt, and young children must not travel in the front seats. The quality of the roads varies greatly, and care is required at all times. Beware of large and unexpected potholes and unmarked sharp bends on mountain roads. A programme of erecting attractive stone barriers is currently under way on those roads which have sheer drops on both sides. Progress in these mountain areas can be very slow so allow more time than usual for whatever distance you have to travel. Let local traffic pass when safe to do so. There are two stretches of motorway on the island, Santa Cruz to Puerto de la Cruz (*Autopista del Norte*) and Santa Cruz to Reina Sofía Airport (*Autopista del Sur*).

Buy a good map before setting out to explore the island as the road markings and sign-posting are often inadequate, and it is easy to miss turnings. Stick to main roads as tracks which seem to be in good condition can quickly deteriorate.

Towns can often be busy and congested so care is also required here. The speed limit in towns is 40 kph, on other main roads 90 kph, and on motorways 120 kph. Crash-helmets must be worn on motorbikes. In the country the *Guardia Civil* deal with traffic offenders and are very strict. In the towns the *Policía Municipal* exercise control. See **Police**.
See **Garages**, **Parking**, **Petrol**.

Eating Out: See RESTAURANTS, **Restaurants**.

Electricity: Mainly 220V with round-pin, two-point plugs, so that adaptors are normally required for UK appliances. These are available in most large supermarkets at about 350-400ptas.

Emergencies:
Police - Tel: 091 (for all emergencies).
Fire - Tel: 22.00.80 (Santa Cruz), 33.00.80 (Puerto de la Cruz).
Ambulance - Tel: 28.18.00 (Santa Cruz), 38.38.12 (Puerto de la Cruz).
Emergency Medical Services - Tel: 24.15.02 (Santa Cruz),
38.38.12 (Puerto de la Cruz).
See also **Crime and Theft**, **Health**.

Esperanza Forest: An impressive forest with a variety of trees, including pine and eucalyptus, and with a good road leading up along the central spine of the island from La Laguna (see **A-Z**) to Las Cañadas (see EXCURSION 2, WALK 4, **A-Z**). The several excellent view-points are ideal for picnics.

Events: There are numerous festivals in Tenerife throughout the year. Some of the more colourful and popular ones include:
January - 5th & 6th *Cabalgada de los Reyes Magos* (Procession of the Three Kings) at Santa Cruz.
February - The Carnival starts six weeks before Lent and is preceded by the election of the carnival queen. There follows two weeks of dancing in the streets, music and costumed processions in Santa Cruz and other parts of the island.
March - Holy Week parades, especially interesting at La Laguna and Santa Cruz.
May and June - Corpus Christi processions, particularly in La Orotava and La Laguna, where marvellous carpets are made out of flowers and sand.
June - The *Romería de San Isidro*, a costumed pilgrimage from San Isidro to La Orotava, with carts drawn by bullocks; 24th *Fiesta de San Juan* at Icod de los Vinos.

July - 1st Sunday *Romería de San Benito Abad*, a costumed parade with ox-drawn carts at La Laguna; *Fiesta del Mar*, a combination of secular water sports and religious ceremonies at Santa Cruz and Puerto de la Cruz: 16th *Fiesta de la Virgen del Carmen* at Santa Cruz.

August - 15th *Romería de la Virgen de la Candelaria* where the appearance of the Virgin to the Guanches is re-enacted. See **Nuestra Señora de la Candelaria**.

September - The *Fiestas del Santísimo Cristo*. Processions, drama, sport, cultural displays and poetry readings at La Laguna and Tacoronte. See also **Music**.

Excursions: Organized coach trips to all parts of Tenerife are readily available, departing from the main towns. The most popular tours include Mount Teide (see **EXCURSION 2**, **WALK 4**, **A-Z**), the Anaga Mountains (see **EXCURSION 3**, **A-Z**), the shops of Santa Cruz (see **SHOPPING 1**), and exotic nightspots such as La Cueva (see **NIGHTLIFE 2**). The Donkey Safari from Arafo is a more unusual treat. The coastal towns provide a choice of boat trips, short excursions around Tenerife itself, and longer cruises to the other islands. Air travel within the Canaries is relatively inexpensive, and a day trip to La Palma or Gran Canaria (see **ISLANDS, A-Z**) is feasible on a moderate budget. The coast of North Africa is also within easy reach.

Fernández de Lugo, Alonso (1456-1525): A nobleman from Andalucía entrusted with the task of subjecting the Canary Islands to Spanish rule in the late 15thC. He founded the town of Las Palmas on Gran Canaria (see **ISLANDS, A-Z**) in 1487, and went on to invade Tenerife on 1 May, 1492, landing at what is now Santa Cruz. It took him four years to conquer the island and he established the town of La Laguna (see **A-Z**) as capital in 1496. He also introduced the parallel grid street system.

Food: Apart from the familiar Spanish dishes such as *paella* you will also find food more typical of the Canary Islands:

Gofio - dating from Guanche times (see **A-Z**), a mixture of roasted corn or oat flour with water, and added to sauces or served as an accompaniment to various dishes.

Puchero - a dish resembling the French *pot au feu*; vegetables stewed with meat, usually pork or veal.

Sancocho - fish and potatoes with a variety of sauces.

Conejo en salmorejo - rabbit served in a spicy sauce.

Mojo picón - another tangy sauce, accompanying fish or meat.

Mojo verde - less strong than

mojo picón, and with a herbal flavour.

Fresh fish, whether fried, grilled or boiled, is on nearly every menu. Sole and tuna are popular, and the local favourites include *vieja, corvina* and *cherne.*

Also worth trying is the delicious and distinctive goat's milk cheese, another local product.

Tapas are an excellent way of sampling different dishes - order some with your drinks, and your snack may consist of shrimps, fried squid, mushrooms and other local specialities.

Fuerteventura: The nearest of all the Canary Islands to the coast of Africa, and possessing the longest coastline. With its wide stretches of sand and numerous beaches, it is a haven for those who enjoy swimming, scuba diving, windsurfing and fishing. There is little in the way of nightlife, so Fuerteventura is also ideal for those simply seeking peace and quiet. The island reaches its highest point of 800 m at the Peninsula de Jandía in the south west. Places of interest include the coastal town of Corralejo and the island's historical capital of Betancuria, named after Jean de Bethencourt (see **A-Z**). See **ISLANDS**.

Garachico: 26 km west of Puerto de la Cruz. Garachico, formerly an important port on the north coast, was largely destroyed by a volcanic eruption in 1706. It was rebuilt on a semi-circular mass of lava protruding into the sea and has managed to retain much of its original charm. Older buildings include the 17thC palace of the Marquis of Adeje and the Iglesia de Santa Ana which houses some important works by the Canarian sculptor, Luján Pérez (1756-1815). The 16thC Castillo de San Miguel, situated on the seafront, is also worth a visit. See **EXCURSION 1**.

Garages: They are numerous throughout the island and generally provide a satisfactory service. If spare parts are not available for your make of car, long delays in completing repairs are inevitable.

Gomera: The closest island to Tenerife and usually visible from the west coast. It has a rocky coastline and mountainous interior. Gomera is famous for *silbo,* the unique whistling language the locals use to

communicate with each other from hilltop to hilltop, often over consid-
erable distances. *Silbo* is sadly dying out as a living language, but has
been retained as a unique tourist attraction.

The capital town of San Sebastián has a population of 7000. From here
Christopher Columbus (see **A-Z**) set off on his journey to America in
1492, a fact commemorated by a national monument in the former
fortress of Torre del Conde. The verdant Valle Hermigua to the east of
the island and the terraced slopes of the Valle Gran Rey contain the
most striking scenery on the island.

The ferry to San Sebastián from Los Cristianos on Tenerife is often
crowded with visitors, but Gomera has no airport, so tourism has had a
limited effect on the islanders' peaceful way of life.
See **EXCURSION 5, ISLANDS**.

Gran Canaria: Situated between Tenerife and Fuerteventura (see
ISLANDS, A-Z), Gran Canaria is an island of stark contrasts, with mountains, arid plains, tropical vegetation, cliffs, ravines and fertile valleys.
It is an increasingly popular and busy destination for holiday makers.
The capital, Las Palmas, offers museums, churches and an old quarter
of typical Canarian buildings to wander through at your leisure, as well
as a bustling social life of nightclubs and restaurants. There are also
some fine beaches, notably at Maspalomas. See **ISLANDS**.

Guanches: When the first explorers arrived on the islands in the
13thC, the Guanches were comparable to a Stone Age people, with
only rudimentary tools and utensils, an apparent absence of written
language (though some undeciphered symbols have been discovered),
and natural cave dwellings formed in the lava flows. They kept goats,
sheep, pigs and dogs, and their diet consisted mainly of *gofio* (see
Food), meat and goat's cheese. Guanche society was patriarchal, with a
king (*Mencey*) at the head of the territorial units, of which there were
eight on Tenerife at the time of the Spanish conquest in the 15thC. It is
thought that they were sun and moon worshippers. Evidence of a con-
vent of priestesses has been found on Gran Canaria (see **ISLANDS, A-Z**).
One of the most fascinating aspects of Guanche culture is the fact that
they mummified their dead - a practice otherwise known only to the

Egyptians and Peruvians. The bodies were left to dry in the sun, treated with herbs and ointments, and then wrapped in skins. They were then left, with their possessions, in virtually inaccessible caves. This practice suggests that they held a belief in life after death.

The Museo Arqueológico in Santa Cruz (see **WALK 1**, **WHAT TO SEE 1**) provides an interesting background to Guanche culture, with displays of artefacts and historical findings from the island.

Hairdressers: There are plenty of hairdressers in the bigger towns and tourist resorts, and the quality and price is much the same as in Europe. For men a good cut costs between 2000 and 3000ptas, and for women between 3000 and 6000ptas depending on styling.

Men - Olympo, Plaza de la Candelaria, Santa Cruz. Tel: 24.37.12.

Women - Lucy, c/ General Sanjurjo 16, Santa Cruz. Tel: 27.09.55.

Halamy, c/ San Juan, Puerto de la Cruz. Tel: 38.20.24.

Health: Before leaving for Tenerife, EC residents can obtain form E111 entitling them to free medical attention while on holiday. It is also advisable to take out health insurance whilst booking your holiday to cover the expense of extensive treatment and emergency travel home.

General Hospital - Carretera del Norte (between Santa Cruz and La Laguna). Tel: 64.10.11/64.63.12.

Children's Hospital - c/ Carmen Monteverde 47, Santa Cruz.
Tel: 28.65.50.

Most doctors speak some English. Some addresses are:

Dr John Hebditch, 60 Edfo Azul, Urb. Arco Iris, Los Cristianos.
Tel: 79.44.21.

Dr Hengst-Theis, Edfo Iders - Apto 302, Avenida del Generalísimo 28, Puerto de la Cruz. Tel: 38.10.62.

The most common medical problems experienced by tourists are brought on by an excess of food, drink and exposure to the sun, so moderation is advised if you don't want to spoil your holiday. Also be prepared for variations in weather conditions when travelling around the island, especially if walking.

Hierro: This tiny triangular island consists of a central plateau culmi-

nating in the summit of Mount Mal Paso at 1320 m, and open coast to the north forming a 14 km bay, El Golfo. The charming county town of Valverde has a population of 5000, and its 18thC fortified church contains an admirable statue of the Virgin.

In the 17thC the westernmost tip of Hierro, La Punta de Orchilla, was designated the original prime meridian (0 degrees longitude), as the island was considered to be the end of the world. It was from Hierro that Columbus (see **A-Z**) set sail for his second voyage of discovery to the New World in 1493. See **ISLANDS**.

Icod de los Vinos: 22 km west of Puerto de la Cruz. A pleasant town in the centre of an area noted for wine and banana production. It contains the most famous dragon tree or *drago* on the island (see **WHAT TO SEE 4, A-Z**), which is carefully tended and attracts many sightseers. Also of interest are the 15th/16thC Iglesia de San Marcos, with its Renaissance facade, and the adjacent San Franciscan monastery. See **EXCURSION 1, WHAT TO SEE 4**.

Information: See **Tourist Information**.

Insurance: Before going on holiday, visitors are advised to take the usual precautions to protect themselves from expenses incurred by theft, accident or ill-health.

Jardín Botánico: One of the most comprehensive collections of tropical plants in the world, displayed in just two and a half hectares of gardens at Carretera del Botánico in Puerto de la Cruz. The Marquis Villanueva de Prado founded the gardens in 1788 under the orders of King Charles III of Spain and it flourished in the climate of the Canaries. An immense rubber tree, over 200 years old, stands on a tangle of roots. Orchids thrive in the greenhouse, there's a cactus corner, and a profusion of flowers and bird-song add to the atmosphere. At the entrance brochures in English are on sale. See **WHAT TO SEE 3**.

La Laguna: 8 km west of Santa Cruz. A university and cathedral town, its full name is San Cristóbal de la Laguna, and it is Tenerife's second largest town, after Santa Cruz. Founded in the late 15thC by the Spanish conqueror, Alonso Fernández de Lugo (see **A-Z**), and the capital of the island until 1723, it is designed on a grid street system. La Laguna boasts some fine examples of colonial architecture and is famous for its Corpus Christi celebrations in May and June, when carpets of sand and petals are laid in the street (see **Events**). It has retained much of its original character and exists independently of the tourism which characterizes many of the island's larger towns and resorts. See **EXCURSION 3, WALK 2, WHAT TO SEE 2.**

La Laguna Cathedral: Founded in the 16thC and rebuilt in the early 20thC with a Neoclassical facade and well-proportioned elegant pseudo-Gothic interior. It houses a fine statue of St Christopher by Fernando Estévez (1788-1854) and a sculpted marble pulpit (1767). Other features include a splendid organ (London, 1857) and Neoclassical choir stalls. The most striking work of art is the enormous Baroque altarpiece, La Virgen de los Remedios, flanked by Flemish paintings and set off by a richly-embossed silver altar. See **EXCURSION 3, WALK 2, WHAT TO SEE 2.**

Lanzarote: The most distinctly volcanic island of the archipelago, with its preponderance of lava fields splashed with the colour of the local vegetation. This grows in remarkable abundance thanks to an ingenious agricultural method which uses the thin layers of volcanic ash to create the necessary moisture for plants to grow. Lanzarote is largely flat and therefore there is a constant refreshing breeze blown in from the shores of Africa. The island's attractions include camel rides up into the volcanic range of Montañas de Fuego (Fire Mountains), coastal caves and lagoons, and some extensive beaches such as Playa Blanca. See **ISLANDS.**

La Orotava: 8 km south of Puerto de la Cruz. One of the oldest towns on the island, nestling among the banana plantations of the valley, and now a major crafts centre. The Casa de los Balcones has superbly-carved wooden balconies and a display of embroidery work in its patio. It was in La Orotava that the tradition started of creating unique works of art from flowers and sand for the Corpus Christi celebrations (see **Events**). The parish church of Nuestra Señora de la Concepción (see **A-Z**) has an impressive facade and contains many treasures, and the Hospital de la Santísima Trinidad offers a splendid view of the valley below. See **EXCURSION 1, WHAT TO SEE 4**.

La Palma: Compared to other islands of its size, La Palma boasts some of the world's highest peaks and one of the largest known volcanic craters, La Caldera de Taburiente (770 m deep and 28 km in circumference), now a national park and covered in pine woods. The capital, Santa Cruz de La Palma, has a population of 15,000 and is located on the eastern coast. The picturesque houses and magnificent examples of 16thC architecture, as seen in the Town Hall and church of San Salvador, make it a charming town to visit. La Palma's economy is based on bananas, tobacco and cigars, and its activities as a port. Tourism is also rapidly expanding. See **EXCURSION 4, ISLANDS**.

Las Cañadas: An old volcanic crater formed millions of years ago and made into a national park in 1954. The exterior ridge is made up of steep craggy walls, and encloses a chaotic and arid plateau of strange

rock formations and gravel plains 2215m above sea level. It measures 16 km across and 45 km round the perimeter. The most recent volcanic activity was at the end of the 18thC.

The Centro de Visitantes near El Portillo to the north-east of the crater (open 0900-1600) provides film shows, photos, samples, explanations of how the crater is thought to have been formed, and guided walks by arrangement. For further information contact the Information Service at La Laguna. Tel: 25.99.03/26.38.98. See **EXCURSION 2**, **Parque Nacional del Teide**.

Las Raíces: An obelisk in a clearing of La Esperanza forest (see **A-Z**) which marks the spot where an event took place that was to dramatically effect the history of Spain. Here, in June 1936, General Franco held a meeting of military leaders to determine their loyalty in supporting him against the government. See **EXCURSION 2**.

Los Cristianos: 75 km south-west of Santa Cruz. A new and bustling resort built around an old port, and now merging along the

coastline with neighbouring Playa de las Américas (see **A-Z**). There are numerous shops and inexpensive restaurants. The beach is well maintained and offers all forms of water sports. Its shallow waters are ideal for children (see **BEACHES 1**). From the port it is possible to take the ferry to visit the island of Gomera. See **EXCURSION 5**, **ISLANDS**, **A-Z**.

Los Gigantes: 55 km west of Puerto de la Cruz. A pleasant town on the west coast, set beneath the impressive cliffs of the same name. It has an air of prosperity and consists mainly of private villas and time-share apartments. There is a yachting marina lined by restaurants, shops and cafés, and a small beach of black sand where pedalos are available for hire. Both Los Gigantes and nearby Puerto de Santiago offer the chance of quiet and relaxing holidays. See **EXCURSION 1**.

Los Realejos: 6 km west of Puerto de la Cruz. A town comprised of two settlements, Realejo Alto and Realejo Bajo, originally the camps of the opposing armies of the Guanches (see **A-Z**) and the Spanish Conquistadores, and the site of Tenerife's last battle in 1496. Los Realejos contains one of the oldest churches on the island, Iglesia de Santiago, built by order of the conquering Andalusian nobleman, Alonso Fernández de Lugo (see **A-Z**). The church houses three painted panels thought to be by the Anvers School (16thC). See **EXCURSION 1**.

Markets: The big fruit and vegetable market in Santa Cruz is called Nuestra Señora de África (see **WHAT TO SEE 1**). It offers colourful displays of local produce, with fish on sale in the basement. Most villages have their own market day - enquire at local tourist offices. There is also a weekly flea market at La Orotava (see **A-Z**).

Money: There are numerous *bureaux de change* which keep roughly the same opening times (see **A-Z**) as shops. Hotels offer the same rate of exchange for money as banks. See **Banks**, **Credit Cards**, **Currency**, **Traveller's Cheques**.

Moped and Motorbike Hire: Mopeds and motorbikes are a good way to see the island and it is possible to hire them at most beach resorts. For a Vespino the cost is about 1000ptas per day (reduced to 800ptas daily for 7-day hire). A Suzuki 750 would cost around 2500ptas per day. Insurance is an additional 300-500ptas per day. Tenerife's roads vary greatly in quality and the volume of traffic carried, from remote and steep mountain tracks to fast main routes. Experience and caution are essential.

Motos Santos - c/ Playa Azul, Playa de las Americás. Tel: 79.16.39.

Rosema - c/ de Méndez Núñez 49, Santa Cruz. Tel: 48.04.64.

Mount Teide: At 3718 m, the highest mountain in Spain, a volcanic crater last active at the end of the 18thC. Mount Teide was formed after a number of eruptions, by Chahorra in particular, and rose out of the crater, La Rambleta. During the winter months the peak is often snow-capped, providing an unusual background to the sun-baked plains of the south. It is possible to walk up to the edge of the crater (50 m in diameter, 25 m deep) from the terminus of the cable car at 3555 m. This is a popular excursion and queues for the cable car can be lengthy. It may be best either to make an early start and arrive before the first run at 0900 or wait until mid-afternoon when the queues have often shortened. The last cable car is at 1600. Strong winds can prevent it from operating, so check the weather before departing. The cable car also carries a warning against use by those suffering from heart disease. See **EXCURSION 2**, **Parque Nacional del Teide**.

Music: Tenerife has its own symphony orchestra. The season is from October to April with concerts in the Parque San Francisco in Puerto de la Cruz. For tickets and information about concerts, contact: Oficinas del Parque San Francisco, c/ Agustín de Bethencourt, Puerto de la Cruz. Tel: 38.36.20.

The music festival takes place in January and lasts for one month, with concerts at the Teatro Guimero in Santa Cruz and the university in La Laguna. For information, contact: Patronata Insular de Música, Cabildo de Tenerife, Plaza de España 1, Santa Cruz. Tel: 24.20.90.

Canary Island folk music, with its Spanish and Latin American influences, mixes lively songs and dances with slower melodies. Groups such as the Taburiente, Los Majuelos and the Sabandeños have led a

revival in traditional music, and the Canaries have their own unique musical creation, the small stringed instrument known as a *timple*.

Nelson, Horatio (1758-1805): The famous British admiral sailed into Santa Cruz in Tenerife in 1797 in an attempt to capture a Spanish treasure ship said to be lying in the harbour. 226 sailors died in the unsuccessful assault, and Nelson lost his arm and was forced to retreat. The flags of his ships are preserved in Nuestra Señora de la Concepción in Santa Cruz (see **WALK 1, WHAT TO SEE 1, A-Z**), and the famous cannon, El Tigre (reputed to be the one which injured Nelson), can be seen at the military museum, Castillo de Paso Alto in Santa Cruz (see **WHAT TO SEE 1**).

Newspapers: Many foreign newspapers are on sale in the main towns and resorts the day after publication. Apart from the regional Spanish papers, there is also the *Diaros de Avisos*, a daily newspaper with an English and German edition every two weeks. See **What's On**.

Nuestra Señora de la Candelaria: According to legend, a statue of the Virgin was washed up on the shores of Candelaria in the 14thC and became an object of worship for the Guanches (see **A-Z**), who were unaware of its Christian significance. It was housed in a cave (today known as San Blas) and later in a sanctuary near the present church where it was venerated until 1826 when it was carried out to sea by a tidal wave. The statue seen today, and housed in the sumptuous Basílica de Nuestra Señora de la Candelaria, is a copy carved by Fernando Estévez soon after the loss of the original. It attracts many pilgrims from all over the Canaries every August (see **Events**). See **WHAT TO SEE 4, Candelaria**.

Nuestra Señora de la Concepción (La Laguna): This early 16thC church is one of the most beautiful churches on the island. Crowned by a six-tiered tower, it is built in typical Canarian style with three naves, and features a magnificent Mudejar wood ceiling and a 17thC sculptured Baroque pulpit. Amongst its many treasures are several statues by Fernando Estévez (1788-1854) and some unique 15thC varnished ceramic baptismal fonts. See **EXCURSION 3, WHAT TO SEE 2**.

Nuestra Señora de la Concepción (La Orotava): Behind the twin-towered Baroque facade of this 18thC church stands a remarkable high altar fashioned out of marble and alabaster by the Italian sculptor, Giuseppe Gagini. Other works of art are the 17thC Baroque altarpiece of the Virgin sculpted in wood by Lázaro Gonzales, and several examples of 18th and 19thC Canarian sculpture, including work by Luján Pérez (1756-1815). See **EXCURSION 1, WHAT TO SEE 4**.

Nuestra Señora de la Concepción (Santa Cruz): Originally built in the 16thC, the church was destroyed by fire in the 17thC and required extensive renovation. Today's building is largely of the 18thC and consists of a low nave with four aisles. The marble pulpit encrusted with jasper is particularly fine, as is the richly worked high altar with a sculpture by Luján Pérez (1756-1815) depicting the Virgin Mary grieving for Christ. There are also several paintings dating from the 17th to the 19thC. Amongst other treasures are the flags captured from Nelson

(see **A-Z**) after his defeat in 1797 and relics of the conquest of Tenerife by Alonso Fernández de Lugo (see **A-Z**). See **WALK 1, WHAT TO SEE 1**.

Opening Times: They vary greatly, but generally:
Shops - 0900/0930-1300 & 1600/1630-1930 Mon.-Sat. in winter and 0900/0930-1300 & 1700-2000 Mon.-Sat. in summer.
Banks - 0900-1400 Mon.-Fri., 0900-1300 Sat.
Post Offices - 0900-1400 Mon.-Fri., 0900-1300 Sat.
Museums - 0900-1300 & 1600-1900 Mon.-Sat., but times vary according to the season, presentation of temporary exhibitions, *etc.* Tourist Offices may be able to help with specific enquiries.
Churches - 0900-1200 & 1700-2000 Mon.-Sat. Again, no set hours, and they also open for services at various times.

Orientation: Tenerife is the largest island in the Canaries (see **A-Z**), an archipelago of seven islands lying just off the west coast of Africa. It has a distinctive three-cornered shape, with the Punta de Anaga in the north east, the Punta de Teno in the north west, and the Punta de la Rasca in the south, forming the three protruding angles. The island is divided along a north-east/south-west axis by a series of mountain ranges starting with the Anaga Mountains (see **A-Z**) in the north west, increasing in altitude to Mount Teide (see **EXCURSION 1, WALK 4, A-Z**) in the centre (3718 m), and then on to the Teno Mountains on the south-west coast. The capital of the island, Santa Cruz (see **A-Z**), lies on the southern slopes of the Anaga massif. There are few rivers, due to the sharp inclination of the mountains and their proximity to the coast. See **ISLANDS**.

Palacio de Carta: Originally built in 1742 by Don Matías Bernardo Carta, general treasurer of the Real Ciudad, the building was bought and restored by the Banco Español de Crédito, and constitutes one of the finest typically Canarian buildings in Santa Cruz. See **WALK 1, WHAT TO SEE 1**.

Parking: Can be difficult in the bigger resorts and towns and it is often wise to leave your car with an attendant, despite the small extra

cost. The international sign (blue 'P' on white background) indicates official car parks.

Parque Nacional del Teide: Consisting of the Las Cañadas crater (see **A-Z**) and Mount Teide itself (see **WALK 4**, **A-Z**), it contains an almost supernatural or lunar landscape which has been used as the location for science fiction films. The area was established as a national park in 1954. Apart from the simple splendour of its scenery, it is also of great geological and botanical interest. The Centro de Visitantes near El Portillo (see **EXCURSION 2**) offers a permanent exhibition covering the history of the area, and produces information leaflets concerning the park's network of walks and footpaths. Guided tours can also be arranged. As a national park, it has various restrictions in force on, *eg* the collection of rock and plant specimens, the lighting of fires and camping. The visitors' centre also advises against tourists undertaking walks and climbs without proper clothing, equipment and supplies.

Petrol: It is cheap, 1500-1700ptas for a full tank, and there are petrol stations in most villages and along the main roads. Outwith the larger resorts and towns you may find that filling stations close during the evenings and all day Sunday.

Pets: You can bring your pet to Tenerife on production of a health certificate and proof of an anti-rabies vaccination within the previous twelve months. The Canarians are not generally animal lovers and you may find problems finding a hotel willing to accommodate your pet. There are veterinary emergency services at:
Can-Fel - Rambla G. Franco 23, Santa Cruz. Tel: 27.63.59.
Consultorio Veterinario - Plaza del Charco, Nieves Ravelo 1, Puerto de la Cruz. Tel: 38.53.37.

Playa de las Américas: 75 km south-west of Santa Cruz. A purpose-built resort on the south-west coast, with a plethora of shopping centres, restaurants, discos, snack bars, amusement arcades and live entertainment aimed largely at the British tourist market. The beaches (see **BEACHES 1**) vary in quality but there are plenty of water sports facili-

ties, and just out of town there is the Aguapark Octopus water playground. A destination for those who like their holidays to be bright and
active, and with plenty of nightlife.

Police: There are three types of police in Spain:
The *Guardia Civil* wear a dark green uniform and distinctive, black
three-cornered hat. They are responsible for offences concerning
national security, *eg* border control, and also serve as traffic police outwith towns. Santa Cruz, tel: 22.31.00. Puerto de la Cruz, tel: 38.35.28.
The *Policía Municipal* wear navy blue uniforms and deal with local
problems and traffic control within towns. Santa Cruz, tel: 092. Puerto
de la Cruz, tel: 38.04.28.
The *Cuerpo Nacional de Policía* deal with serious local crimes, *eg* drugs
and theft. Santa Cruz, tel: 091; Puerto de la Cruz, tel: 38.12.24.
See **Emergencies**.

Post Office: The main post office is in Santa Cruz on the Plaza de
España, tel: 24.20.02. Post offices only deal with letters, parcels and
telegrams - the telephone system is separate (see **A-Z**). Stamps can be
purchased in tobacconists and in most places which sell postcards. It
costs 45ptas to send a postcard and 50ptas for a letter weighing less
than 20 gm. Most post offices are open from 0830-1400 on weekdays
and 0830-1300 on Saturdays.

Public Holidays:
1 January (New Year's Day); 6 January (Epiphany); 2 February
(Candlemas); 19 March (St Joseph's Day); March (Easter); 1 May
(Labour Day); July (Corpus Christi); 25 July (St James' Day); 15 August
(Assumption); 12 October (Discovery of America); 1 November (All
Saints' Day); 8 December (Immaculate Conception); 25 December
(Christmas Day).
In addition to these general public holidays there are local holidays,
festivals and celebrations. See **Events**.

Puerto de la Cruz: 39 km south-west of Santa Cruz. The most
important resort on the north coast of Tenerife, it was founded in the

16thC as La Orotava's port (see **A-Z**) and flourished through the trade in sugar and wine. In later years cochineal and bananas became the main commodities for export. Situated on the coast in front of the luxuriant banana plantations of La Orotava valley, and with the magnificent Mount Teide in the background (see **EXCURSION 2**, **WALK 4**, **Parque Nacional del Teide**, **A-Z**), the town became a favourite winter resort for the British at the turn of the century and has since developed into a thriving, yet dignified, tourist resort. The old port retains much of its original character, in pleasant contrast to the new high-rise hotels and modern shops. There is much of historical interest in the town including the Casa Iriarte, Casa de la Real Aduana, and the 17thC church, Iglesia de la Peña de Francia (see **WALK 3**, **WHAT TO SEE 3**). The Jardín Botánico (see **WALK 3**, **WHAT TO SEE 3**, **A-Z**) houses a unique collection of rare plants which thrive in the Canarian climate. An attractive 20thC development is the Lago de Martiánez, a modern complex of swimming pools designed to make up for the resort's lack of natural beaches. See **BEACHES 2**, **NIGHTLIFE 2**, **RESTAURANTS 2**, **SHOPPING 2**.

Radio and Television: The Canary Island tourist radio station broadcasts in English from Las Palmas on MW 747 khz, Mon.-Sat.

Local Spanish radio stations include Radio Club Tenerife, Radio Cadine, Radio Español and Antenna Tres. The two Spanish TV channels can also be received, with local variations. Occasionally they show foreign films with their original soundtracks, usually late at night. Several of the bars and cafés in modern resorts such as Playa de las Américas (see **A-Z**) show video programmes in English.

Religious Services:

All Saints Anglican Church - Parque Taoro, Puerto de la Cruz.
0930 Sun. (1100 first and third Sun. of each month) and 1000 Wed.
Evangelical Church - c/ Iriarte 6, Puerto de la Cruz. 1000 Sun.
Iglesia de la Peña de Francía - Plaza de la Iglesia, Puerto de la Cruz.
International Mass, mostly in English, 1000 Sun.

Restaurants: For authentic Canarian cooking leave the buffet meals served in hotels and try one of the many restaurants around the island. In Santa Cruz and Puerto de la Cruz it is possible to sample a wide variety of different dishes, and the establishments in the smaller towns usually provide a good choice of local cuisine. For a dinner of fresh fish try one of the restaurants overlooking the port at Los Abrigos.
Grading of restaurants theoretically works on a 'fork' system, five forks signifying the highest grade - but in reality it is best to follow the example of the locals in looking for good food, regardless of the decor of the establishment. It is usual to leave a 5% to 10% tip if you are satisfied with your meal and the service. The bigger towns have adapted to the demands of tourists and start serving in the evening at 1900 or 2000, but in the smaller villages it is still customary to eat later, at about 2200. Approximate price ranges for a full dinner are 1000-1500ptas (budget), 1500-3000ptas (moderate), 3000-6000ptas (expensive). See **RESTAURANTS**.

Santa Cruz: 39 km north-east of Puerto de la Cruz. Modern-day capital of Tenerife and of the province which incorporates La Palma, Gomera and Hierro (see **ISLANDS**, **A-Z**), and site of the island's administrative institutions and military headquarters. It has a population of 200,000, slightly less than Las Palmas, rival capital of the eastern province. One of Spain's biggest and most important ports, its main claim to historical fame is as the site of the battle of 1797 in which Horatio Nelson (see **A-Z**) lost his right arm and was forced to retreat. El Tigre, the cannon which fired the shot, is still preserved in the military museum at Castillo de Paso Alto. See **WHAT TO SEE 1**.

Santa Cruz is an important port and busy shopping centre but retains a Colonial flavour with its housing adorned by carved wooden balconies so typical of Canarian architecture. The centre of the town is dominated by the magnificent square, Plaza de España (see **WALK 1**), with its Monument to the Fallen of the Spanish Civil War (1936-1939). Leading up from this is the Plaza de la Candelaria and the shopping precinct of Calle de Castillo, and beyond this lies the extensive grounds of the city's municipal park, the Parque García Sanabria (see **WHAT TO SEE 1**). As befits a capital, Santa Cruz also contains some fine churches, as well as museums and an art gallery. In February the city hosts the spectacular carnival with costumed parades and displays of dancing. See **NIGHTLIFE 1, RESTAURANTS 1, SHOPPING 1, Events**.

Santísimo Cristo de la Laguna: Brought to Tenerife by Alonso Fernández de Lugo (see **A-Z**) in 1520, this statue is housed in the 1513 Santuario del Cristo, a former Franciscan chapel (see **WHAT TO SEE 2**). It is a fine work of art - an ornate black oak statue dating from the 15th/16thC, and attributed to an anonymous artist of the Seville School. The Christ is displayed above the altar of the church in an embossed silver frame and is one of the island's most venerated pieces, the object of a pilgrimage every year on 14th September. See **WALK 2**.

Shopping: The best place to shop for items benefitting from the low tax system is Santa Cruz. There is a multitude of shops and bazaars along the Calle de Castillo. These are often run by Indians who speak English, Spanish and German. Always check quality and guarantees before making a purchase. It is wise to go to one of the big department stores first to get an idea of what is available. Bargaining can be an acceptable practice in the smaller shops where prices are not marked.

A choice of craftwork is available in both Santa Cruz and Puerto de la Cruz, though it is often more interesting to buy pieces from the smaller villages. Puerto de la Cruz is also noted for its choice of furs at reasonable prices.

As is often the case in islands, everyday household goods, food and clothes often have to be imported and can therefore be expensive. There are numerous supermarkets on the island, with small variations in prices, but it is also fun to try shopping for food at the market in Santa Cruz. See **SHOPPING**, **WHAT TO SEE 1**.

Smoking: Tenerife is a smoker's haven as cigarettes and cigars are cheap and there are few public restrictions on smoking. Most brands of foreign cigarettes are available at around 85-100ptas per packet. Canarian cigars are also cheap and plentiful. Because the island is duty-free, the allocation of cigarettes for returning holiday-makers remains at 200 per person, even if you have purchased the goods on the island. See **Customs**.

Sports: A variety of participatory and spectator sports can be enjoyed on Tenerife. For the energetic, there are numerous tennis courts as well as horse riding centres and golf courses, and the countryside affords many enjoyable walks and climbs (see **WALKS**, **Walking**). Most sporting activity is based around the sea, however. If you are interested in more than just swimming, the main resorts also provide facilities for diving, sailing, windsurfing, fishing, *etc.* Or why not join in one of the many beach games?

Of the local spectator sports, bullfighting (see **A-Z**) is an exotic attraction to some visitors, while Canarian wrestling (see **A-Z**) is also of interest. Soccer is the big favourite with the islanders, and most towns have a playing field. The main stadium is the Estadio H. Rodríguez López, off Calle San Sebastián in Santa Cruz.

Taxis: Taxis can be identified by a green light at night or a green *libre* sign displayed on windscreens during the day. The flag-down charge is 55ptas and the journey is charged at 30ptas per km. It costs 650ptas per hr to ask a taxi to wait for you. Not all taxis are metered and it is best to negotiate a price in advance for excursions or longer trips.

Telephones and Telegrams: Telephone boxes are plentiful and those marked *Internacional* can be used to phone abroad. They take 5, 25, 50 and 100pta coins and clear instructions in English, French and German are provided. To phone abroad first dial 07 and, when you hear a change in the dialling tone, enter the appropriate international code (*eg* UK 44, USA 01). Then dial the area code (without the initial 0) and the rest of the number. There are also very convenient public telephone offices, identified by the sign of a blue telephone, where the fee is paid at the desk after the call is made. Charges are the same. Hotels, however, charge an additional 10-20% tax on phone calls.
Telegrams can be sent either by telephone or through the Post Office (see **A-Z**), which in Santa Cruz also has fax and telex facilities.

Television: See **Radio and Television**.

Tipping: Whilst tipping is not always necessary (a service charge is normally included in bills), it is becoming customary. If you are happy with the service, leave approximately 10% for taxi drivers, waiters, guides and hairdressers, and about 50ptas for the hotel porter.

Toilets: There are few public toilets on the island. You may go into a bar or café and ask for *servicios*, and you are expected to buy something such as a glass of wine or cup of coffee, out of courtesy.

Tourist Information: In Santa Cruz there are two tourist offices offering friendly advice from staff fluent in English, French and German. Maps, brochures and free posters are available. Tenerife is still in the process of developing its tourist industry, and this is reflected in the fact that some events are poorly publicized and even tourist office staff may be unaware of specific opening times, prices, *etc*. They are, however, planning to install a simple-to-use computerized information system at the airports and main resorts, and this should improve the situation.
Santa Cruz - Palacio Insular, Plaza de España, tel: 24.25.93.
Open 0800-1500 Mon.-Fri., 0900-1300 Sat.

c/ La Marina 57, tel: 28.38.53. Open 0800-1500.
Puerto de la Cruz - Plaza de la Iglesia 3, tel: 38.60.00.
Open 0800-1400.

Transport: There are no trains on Tenerife but the bus services are generally good, although the roads themselves vary in quality in the rural districts. Boats also provide occasional links between the major resorts. Transport between the islands is relatively inexpensive by air, a good alternative to the fairly long ferry journeys if time is limited. The 80 min hydrofoil trip from Santa Cruz to Las Palmas on Gran Canaria (see **ISLANDS**, **A-Z**) is a special attraction.
See **Airports**, **Buses**, **Car Hire**, **Driving**, **Moped and Motorbike Hire**, **Taxis**.

Traveller's Cheques: Many hotels will exchange traveller's cheques, but they offer less favourable terms than banks. You will require your passport for transactions concerning traveller's cheques.

Vegetation: The flora on the Canary Islands varies according to the altitude and the localized climate. More than 30% of the species are unique to the islands, and authentic survivors from the Tertiary era can be found, for example *laurelsilva* or laurelwood, which is impossible to find outwith the archipelago.
In the arid, low-lying regions of Tenerife (particularly the south) the vegetation includes cacti and palm trees. Dragon trees (see **Drago**) also

grow at fairly low altitudes. In the centre and north the flora is distribut-
ed in ascending layers, with laurelwood giving way to bog-myrtle and
briar. Above 1000 m pines appear, including the *pinus Canariensis,* a
fire-resistant species which provides much of the wood used in the
manufacture of the carved balconies to be seen all over the island.
Agriculture is still one of the main sources of income, and banana plantations (see **A-Z**), vineyards and tobacco fields are to be seen in the valley regions. Flowers are grown in abundance in the lusher parts of the
island, adding wonderful splashes of colour.

Walking: Among the best of the many regions of Tenerife which offer
marvellous countryside for walking are the Parque Nacional del Teide
(see **EXCURSION 2**, **A-Z**), the Anaga Mountains (see **EXCURSION 3**, **A-Z**)
and the Teno mountain range (see **EXCURSION 1**).
A gentler walk is to be found along the Barranco del Infierno (see **A-Z**).
Walkers should take care to equip themselves properly to cope with the
often rough terrain and the variable climate at higher altitudes. See
WALKS.

What's On: There are two monthly magazines printed mainly for
British residents on the island, but also containing useful information
about local events, eating out, where to go and what to do. They are
the *Island Gazette* (220ptas) and *Tenerife Today* (200ptas), both available
from international bookshops and some kiosks.
There is also a booklet called *Guía Práctica* which comes out every six
months or so, and includes practical information about buses, events,
postal rates, *etc.* It is written in Spanish, English, French and German.

Wrestling, Canarian: *Lucha Canaria* is a sport originating in
ancient Egyptian or Guanche times (see **A-Z**). Two barefoot contestants
face each other within a circle of 10 m in diameter. The aim is to grasp
one's adversary and throw him to the ground. Much ritual precedes the
contest and the scoring system is sufficiently complicated to make it
difficult for the uninitiated to predict the winner before the judge
announces his decision. Demonstrations of Canarian wrestling are held
regularly and are a popular feature of some fiestas.